SLOW COOKING
In Crock-Pot, Slow Cooker, Oven and Multi-Cooker

Joanna White

BRISTOL PUBLISHING ENTERPRISES, INC.
San Leandro, California

A Nitty Gritty® cookbook

Printed in the United States of America.

ISBN 1-55867-100-5

Cover design: Frank Paredes
Cover photography: John Benson
Food stylist: Suzanne Carreiro
Illustrator: James Balkovek

CONTENTS

SLOW COOKING: TIPS AND TRICKS

Slow cookers are ideal for today's busy lifestyles. Prepare the recipe the night before or in the morning, put the cooker on before you leave and have your meal ready to eat when you get home after a long day. Count the advantages and you'll go back to that slow cooker in your cupboard, or invest in a new one.

When I first began this project, I reviewed the handful of books currently available on the subject of slow cooking (sometimes called Crock-Pot cooking). Many of those books have recipes similar to each other. My goal was to present the reader with a new collection of delicious slow cooking recipes that not only provide variety, but are in tune with today's thinking about food. I hope you enjoy them.

THE ADVANTAGES OF SLOW COOKING

- A slow cooker allows the cook to prepare the meal in advance.

- More nutrients are retained because of the lower temperatures used.

- One-pot meals cut down on cleanup.

- Food is generally more juicy because slow cooking seals in moisture.
- Considerably less energy is used (less than a 100-watt bulb) when cooking on low.
- Less space is needed to cook food. Slow cooking is ideal for boats, R.V.s, cabins and small kitchens.
- When using the low setting, you can leave without worry about having to tend the food. Low heat will not dry out or burn the food. Generally, you do not even have to stir.
- Slow cookers are ideal even in the summer because they do not heat up the kitchen.
- Exact timing is not crucial, so if you are delayed at work, your food will not be overdone.
- Slow cookers are ideal for buffets and informal entertaining because they allow you to serve directly from the pot. Use as you would a chafing dish to keep food warm or to serve hot drinks.

DO'S AND DON'TS OF SLOW COOKING

- Do not take the lid off during the cooking process unless the recipe calls for it.

This will let out steam which is used to cook the food at the top of the pot and it will take at least 15 minutes to regain that steam pressure. Also, positively never remove lid during the first 2 hours of baking in the slow cooker.

- Always allow more time when cooking at higher altitudes.

- Always bake on high.

- Low temperature refers to 200° F. High temperature refers to 300° F. If your particular brand of slow cooker has additional settings, be sure to determine where these temperature settings are so you can properly follow the recipes in this book.

- Defrost food before using in recipes. Frozen food may cause the slow cooker to crack if using a porcelain, enamel or crockery-lined pot. Also, frozen food will increase cooking time considerably.

- Be cautious when baking, where another pan is placed in the pot and water is added. Check the pot to make sure the water does not evaporate.

- Do not immerse any electrical control units or parts in water at any time.

- To maintain the finish on the inside of the pot, soak with warm, soapy water and then scrub with a nylon or plastic pad.

- For easier cleanup afterwards, spray inside the pot with nonstick vegetable spray before cooking.

- Root vegetables like carrots, turnips, parsnips, rutabagas, etc., quite often take longer to cook than the meat, so it is best to layer these on the bottom and let the liquid keep the vegetables moist (which helps them cook more evenly).

- Beans are ideal for slow cookers. I like to soak the beans overnight; discard the soaking water and then add the beans to the recipe and slow cook until beans are tender.

- Pasta and rice have a tendency to fall apart or become gummy, so I like to add these ingredients precooked (using conventional cooking methods) at the end of the cooking time or simply serve with the dish.

- Dairy products like milk and sour cream should be added toward the last hour of cooking because slow cooking has a tendency to curdle these products.

- For best results in your slow cooker, fill pot at least half full of ingredients.

METHODS FOR CONVERTING RECIPES TO SLOW COOKERS

- There may be variations in cooking temperatures depending on the particular brand of slow cooker, so first determine the proper LOW (200°) and HIGH

(300°) temperature settings. *NEVER* allow the cooking temperature to drop to less than 180°, in order to prevent spoilage or improperly cooked food.

- Generally quadruple the regular cooking in a slow cooker on low. For example, for a stew which requires 2 to 2½ hours standard cooking time, you would increase the time to 8 to 10 hours on low.

- If choosing to cook on high, double the conventional cooking time but do not leave the slow cooker unattended. You may also need to stir occasionally. 1 hour on HIGH is equivalent to 2 hours on LOW.

- Some brands have very high settings to be used for the purpose of browning meats. After browning, be sure to reduce the temperature to LOW.

- For meats that need browning, such as chicken, slow cook the food first, and then remove and brown in a hot oven or broiler just before serving.

- If you are afraid of not being able to return in time or if cooking time is less than your working day, consider investing in an automatic timer. Your slow cooker plugs into the timer which will turn on automatically after you leave. It is best not have it turn off automatically, because hot food should not be left out more than 2 hours.

- When adapting a recipe to slow cooking, you may need to increase spices.

Because the food tends to lose less liquid from evaporation, the extra juiciness may require additional flavoring.

- Baking requires placing the ingredients in a separate container (like a coffee can, a pudding mold, a tall baking dish, etc.), covering with foil, tying down the foil and surrounding with water.

- For thickening sauces: Turn cooker on high; stir in thickener which has been mixed with cold water and cook 20 to 30 minutes, stirring occasionally until thickened.

  Cornstarch: Use 2 tbs. dissolved in 2 tbs. cold water for every 2 cups of sauce that needs to be thickened.

  Flour: Use 4 tbs. dissolved in 4 tbs. cold water for every 2 cups of sauce that needs to be thickened.

  Tapioca: This is usually stirred in before cooking, so it doesn't need to be mixed with water. Use 3-4 tbs. for every 2 cups of liquid used in the recipe.

  Potato: Sometimes sauces can be thickened by simply adding instant potato flakes or adding pureed potatoes.

TECHNIQUES FOR REDUCING FAT AND SALT IN SLOW COOKING

- Quite often fat is needed to brown meats or onions before cooking. Generally in slow cooking this whole step can be eliminated, so disregard the fat entirely.
- If fat is required to soften the vegetables, try substituting chicken stock or water to wilt vegetables.
- Trim excess fat off meats before cooking.
- For high-fat meats like hamburger and sausage, fry in a skillet and drain off fat before adding to your slow cooker.
- Skim fat off top of pot, if visible, or chill meat mixture; let fat solidify and skim fat off.
- Substitute ground turkey for ground beef to reduce fat.
- The best way to reduce salt in your recipe is to replace with spices or simply increase the quantity of spices already called for in the recipe, so salt is not so necessary.
- One method to reduce saltiness in a recipe is to add chunks of peeled potato which will absorb the salt and remove the chunks before serving the dish.
- Another method to reduce saltiness is to add white pepper (not black). White pepper is more subtle and takes away from the salty flavor.

- Use low salt (or low sodium) canned foods and when the recipe calls for garlic salt or celery salt, use powdered garlic or celery instead (increasing the quantity somewhat).

TYPES OF SLOW COOKERS

I used a variety of slow cookers to test recipes for this book. Slow cookers come in many different shapes and sizes. They range from one solid unit, to separate liners with heating shells, to hot plates with pans on top. Technically, an electric skillet can be used as a slow cooker. Many new versions have deep frying attachments that can reach very high temperatures. A pot that separates from the heating unit for ease of cleaning and storage is a desirable feature.

Slow cooking can also be done in the oven using a casserole, a Dutch oven or other ovenproof container with a tight fitting lid so steam cannot readily escape.

Cook at LOW (200°) by quadrupling the time for conventional stove top cooking. A stew which requires 2 to 2½ hours would be increased to 8 to 10 hours. Cook at HIGH (300°) in the oven by doubling the time.

Be aware that using the oven to cook slowly does not save energy the way a slow cooker pot does and is therefore less economical.

Caring for your slow cooker should be done according to the manufacturer's instructions. Here are some of the surfaces that were used for testing:

Crockery lining. Usually made from glazed stoneware or earthenware, this should be washed (or at least soaked) soon after using. If the slow cooker has a separate liner, it usually can be put in a dishwasher (never immerse the outer electrical unit). Use nylon or plastic scrubbers to get out dried food or stains.

Aluminum lining. I do not advise using aluminum for health reasons and also limitations in cooking high acid foods. If you have one, wash it with soapy water, use nylon pads and always season with oil before using.

Porcelain or baked enamel lining. You need to be a little more cautious in handling this type. Be careful to cool completely before washing. Never use abrasive cleansers, only use nylon scrubbers and rinse very well before heating to avoid staining.

Glass or Corning Ware. This surface is ideal for slow cooking because it absorbs heat rapidly, withstands extreme temperatures and sudden temperatures, is easy to clean and holds heat a long time. Avoid using metal scouring pads.

Stainless steel. Stainless steel is good for heat retention and generally easy to clean. Avoid using steel wool to clean because it can scratch the surface.

Teflon coated. Use nylon or plastic utensils and definitely do not use anything other than nylon or plastic scrubbers. Teflon usually needs to be seasoned before using. If the surface discolors with time, use an appliance stain remover.

APPETIZERS

HONEY CHICKEN WINGS

This is a wonderful appetizer that can be kept warm and served from the slow cooker at a buffet.

3 lb. chicken wings
salt and pepper to taste
1 cup honey
3 tbs. ketchup
½ cup soy sauce
2 tbs. oil
1 clove garlic, minced
sesame seeds for garnish, optional

Disjoint chicken wings and discard tips. Sprinkle wing parts with salt and pepper. Place honey, ketchup, soy sauce, oil and garlic in the slow cooker and stir until mixed well. Add seasoned chicken wings and stir. Set slow cooker on low and cook 5 to 6 hours. If desired, garnish with a sprinkling of sesame seeds.

BARBECUED CHICKEN WINGS

This barbecue sauce is absolutely delicious. Use it with other meats, such as strips of steaks, chicken nuggets, pork medallions, etc.

4 lb. chicken wings
2 large onions, chopped
2 cans (6 oz. each) tomato paste
2 large cloves garlic, minced
¼ cup Worcestershire sauce
¼ cup any variety vinegar
½ cup brown sugar
½ cup sweet pickle relish
½ cup red or white wine
2 tsp. salt
2 tsp. dry mustard

Cut off wing tips and discard. Cut wings at the joint and place in the slow cooker. Add remaining ingredients and stir. Set slow cooker on low and cook for 5 to 6 hours. Serve directly from pot at a buffet with lots of napkins!

BARBECUED CHICKEN DINNER
OR APPETIZER

*This variation of **Barbecued Chicken Wings**, page 12, makes a dinner or a slightly different chicken appetizer.*

3½ lb. whole chicken
1 barbecue sauce recipe from *Barbecued Chicken Wings*

Disjoint chicken and cut into regular serving pieces. Remove skin and all visible fat. Place chicken in the slow cooker and cover with sauce ingredients. Set slow cooker on low and allow chicken to cook for 5 to 6 hours. Carefully remove chicken from pot and pour sauce on top. Or remove chicken from bones and strip into large pieces. Serve with toothpicks as an appetizer.

TERIYAKI CHICKEN WINGS
Makes: about 30 pieces

This is a quick recipe for teriyaki that takes just minutes to prepare. You can also substitute whole skinned chicken pieces for a tender chicken teriyaki dinner.

2 lb. chicken wings
1 small onion, chopped
½ cup light soy sauce
½ cup brown sugar
1 tsp. ground ginger
1-2 cloves garlic, minced
2 tbs. dry sherry

Disjoint chicken wings and discard tips (or use them in stock). Place wing parts in the slow cooker. In a separate bowl, combine onion, soy sauce, sugar, ginger, garlic and sherry. Pour mixture over chicken wings and set slow cooker on low. Cook for approximately 5 to 6 hours. If possible, gently stir halfway through cooking process to insure that all wings are coated with sauce.

HUMMUS DIP

Makes: about 2 cups

Hummus is a Middle Eastern vegetarian dip that has become very popular. I experimented using rehydrated beans versus slow cooked beans and the results were far better with the slow cooker. For variety, add chopped cilantro.

¼ lb. dried garbanzo beans
water to cover beans
1 tbs. olive oil
1 small onion, chopped
2 cloves garlic, minced

½ tsp. turmeric
2 tbs. chopped parsley
salt to taste
1-2 tbs. lemon juice, or more to taste

Rinse dried beans under cold running water. Place in the slow cooker and cover with water, making sure that you have at least 2 inches of water on top of beans. Set cooker on low and allow to cook for 8 to 10 hours. Drain beans; discard water and rinse under cold water. Allow beans to drain well. Place in a food processor or blender and puree until about the consistency of mayonnaise. If mixture appears too coarse, add a little water. In a skillet, heat olive oil and sauté onion and garlic until soft and transparent. Add turmeric and cook an additional minute. Add this mixture to pureed beans in food processor and blend. Add parsley, salt and lemon juice to taste.

HOT ARTICHOKE DIP

Makes: 7-8 cups

This is an incredible dip that goes well with thick, mild-flavored crackers or slices of crusty French bread. Slow cookers are ideal for keeping food warm, especially at buffet parties.

2 jars (14¾ oz. each) marinated artichoke hearts, drained
1 cup mayonnaise, fat-free, if desired
1 cup sour cream, low fat or fat-free, if desired
2 cups grated Parmesan cheese
1 cup chopped water chestnuts
¼ cup finely chopped green onion, or more to taste

Cut artichoke hearts into small pieces. Mix in mayonnaise, sour cream, Parmesan cheese, water chestnuts and green onion. Place in the slow cooker on low for at least 1 hour or until thoroughly heated. Serve directly from slow cooker with crackers or sliced French bread.

CHILI CON QUESO (CHEESE DIP)

Servings: 8

The slow cooker is great for cheese dip because it can be used on a buffet table to keep the cheese warm.

2 tbs. butter
2 tbs. finely chopped onion
1-2 cloves garlic, minced
2 fresh tomatoes, peeled and seeded
4 oz. diced green chilies
2½ cups grated Monterey Jack or cheddar cheese

Turn the slow cooker on high; add butter, onion and garlic and sauté until onion is soft but not brown. Dice tomatoes and add to slow cooker with chilies and cheese. Heat on low for 1 hour or until cheese melts completely. Serve directly from slow cooker with corn chips or sliced French bread.

SPICY BEAN DIP

Makes: 4½ cups

This is a quick and easy vegetarian dip that can be "spiced up" with the addition of jalapeños.

2 cans (16 oz. each) refried beans*
1 pkg. (1¼ oz.) taco seasoning mix
½ cup finely chopped onion
2 cups shredded Monterey Jack or cheddar cheese
several drops Tabasco Sauce
jalapeño peppers to taste, optional

Place refried beans, taco seasoning, onion, cheese and Tabasco in the slow cooker and stir. If you wish to really add heat, carefully remove seeds and chop up jalapeño peppers (be careful not to touch your eyes or face) and stir into bean mixture to your personal taste. If mixture appears too thick, add a little water. Heat on low until mixture is hot and cheese is melted, approximately 1 hour. Serve directly from slow cooker with corn chips, sliced French bread or crackers.

NOTE: To reduce fat, use low fat cheese and increase the seasoning slightly.
*Vegetarian refried beans do not contain animal lard.

HOT BACON AND CHEESE DIP

You can't go wrong with bacon and cheese. I particularly like to serve this with apple and pear slices or thin slices of French bread.

8 slices bacon, diced
8 oz. cream cheese, cubed
2 cups cheddar cheese, shredded
6 tbs. half-and-half
1 tsp. Worcestershire sauce
1/4 tsp. dry mustard
1/4 tsp. onion salt
dash of Tabasco Sauce

Fry finely diced bacon in a skillet until crisp; drain on paper towels and set aside. Place cream cheese, cheddar cheese, half-and-half, Worcestershire sauce, mustard, onion salt and Tabasco in the slow cooker. Set on low and allow cheese to melt slowly, stirring occasionally for approximately 1 hour. Taste and adjust seasonings. Just before guests arrive, stir in bacon and serve directly from slow cooker. If mixture becomes too thick, add more half-and-half to thin. If using apples and pears to accompany this dish, dip fruit slices in lemon juice to help prevent browning.

QUICK AND SIMPLE HAMBURGER DIP

Makes: 5-6 cups

If you are in a pinch and need something quick to fix for impromptu guests, whip this up and keep it warm in the pot. Serve with tortilla chips, plain crackers or thin slices of French bread.

1 lb. extra lean hamburger
½ cup chopped onion
2 cloves garlic, minced
salt to taste
1 can (8 oz.) tomato sauce
¼ cup ketchup
¾ tsp. oregano
1 tsp. sugar
8 oz. cream cheese
⅓ cup grated Parmesan cheese

In a skillet, brown hamburger with onion; discard fat. Pour browned meat and onion into the slow cooker. Add garlic, salt, tomato sauce, ketchup, oregano, sugar, cream cheese and Parmesan. Set cooker on low and serve when cream cheese has melted into mixture, approximately 1 hour. Stir; taste and adjust seasonings.

FAST FRANKFURTER APPETIZERS

Servings: 8-10

This is so simple it is almost embarrassing! I sometimes mix different types of sausages, frankfurters or even hot dogs.

3 lb. frankfurters or precooked sausages
4 tbs. brown sugar
¼ cup water
½ cup whiskey or bourbon
1 cup ketchup

Cut frankfurters or sausages (I like to use a variety like bratwurst, kielbasa, Italian, etc.) into 1-inch pieces. Place frankfurters or sausages in the slow cooker with brown sugar, water, whiskey and ketchup. Set cooker on low for 1 hour; taste and increase ketchup if too strong. Serve directly from pot.

HOT HERBY MUSHROOMS

Servings: 12

For a change from baked mushrooms, try something that is healthy and easy to serve.

6 tbs. butter
1 large onion, chopped
2 tsp. basil
2 tsp. oregano
½ tsp. thyme
¼ cup lemon juice
½ cup sherry
¼ tsp. red pepper flakes
3 lb. mushrooms, washed and left whole

Turn the slow cooker on high. Melt butter; add onion and sauté until onion is limp. Turn cooker on low. Add spices, lemon juice, sherry and pepper flakes and allow mixture to steep on low for 1 to 2 hours. Add mushrooms about 15 minutes before guests arrive. Use toothpicks or a slotted spoon to serve.

HOT CHEESE FONDUE

Beer gives this cheese mixture an unusual zip. Serve with fresh vegetables and corn chips or tortilla chips for dipping. If you really like it hot, add the chopped jalapeño peppers.

1/4 cup flour
2 tsp. chili powder, or to taste
1 lb. Monterey Jack cheese, shredded
1/2 lb. sharp cheddar cheese, shredded
1 can (12 oz.) beer
1 clove garlic, minced
1 can (4 oz.) chopped green chilies
chopped jalapeño peppers to taste, optional

Mix flour with chili powder and toss over shredded cheeses. Pour beer into the slow cooker and cover with shredded cheese mixture. Place garlic, green chilies and jalapeños, if desired, over cheese, but do not stir in until cheese has begun to melt. Set cooker on low; allow to warm slowly and stir occasionally. Serve directly from slow cooker.

HOT BEVERAGES

COFFEE MEDITERRANEAN

This mocha mixture, with a tinge of anise and cinnamon, is served hot with a twist of lemon and orange.

2 qt. hot coffee
1/4 cup chocolate syrup
1/3-1/2 cup sugar
2 sticks (6-inch each) cinnamon
2 tsp. whole cloves
1/2 tsp. anise flavoring
peel of 1 orange, cut into strips for garnish
peel of 1 lemon, cut into strips for garnish
whipped cream for garnish

Combine coffee, chocolate syrup, sugar, cinnamon, cloves and anise flavoring in the slow cooker. Set on low and cook for 45 minutes to 1 hour. Float orange and lemon peel strips which have been tied into knots on top of mixture. Strain liquid into a cup and top each cup with a large dollop of whipped cream.

COFFEE PUNCH

This is a strange combination of coffee, juice and ginger ale that works well together.

6 cups coffee
4 cups apple juice or cider
2 cups apricot brandy
½ tsp. ground ginger
32 oz. ginger ale

Combine coffee, apple juice or cider, apricot brandy and ginger in the slow cooker. Heat on low until hot; add ginger ale and serve immediately.

HOT BRAZILIAN EGGNOG

Usually eggnog is served cold but the Brazilian version is served hot and flavored with coffee.

4 eggs, separated
3 cups milk
2 cups cream
3 tbs. instant coffee
½ cup light corn syrup

½ cup brandy or rum, or to taste
¼ cup water
pinch cinnamon, optional
nutmeg for garnish

With an electric mixer, beat egg yolks lightly; beat in milk, cream, instant coffee and ¼ cup corn syrup. Place mixture in the slow cooker; set on low and cook for half an hour. Stir in brandy or rum. In a saucepan, heat remaining corn syrup and water to a boil and simmer for 5 minutes. Beat egg whites until soft peaks form and slowly pour corn syrup mixture in a thin stream into eggs. Continue beating until soft peaks form again. Fold mixture into hot milk mixture. Ladle into punch cups or mugs and sprinkle with nutmeg.

FRUITED TEA PUNCH

Servings: 12

I like to serve this spicy, warm punch with orange or lemon slices studded with whole cloves.

5 cups apricot nectar
2 cups orange juice
2 cups water
2 tbs. sugar, or more to taste
2 tsp. ground cinnamon
pinch ground cloves
4 tsp. instant tea
1 lemon or orange for garnish
whole cloves for garnish

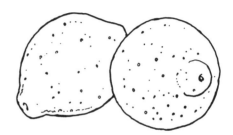

Place apricot nectar, orange juice, water, sugar, cinnamon, and ground cloves in the slow cooker. Heat on low for approximately 1 hour. Stir in tea. Taste and adjust seasoning or sweetness. Cut lemon into slices and stud rind with whole cloves. Serve by pouring into mugs or glasses and floating a slice of studded fruit on top.

TEA NECTAR

This fruity tea punch is refreshing and soothing.

2 qt. boiling water
8 tea bags, regular or herbal
18 oz. unsweetened pineapple juice
12 oz. apricot nectar
1 can (6 oz.) frozen orange juice concentrate, thawed
6 oz. lemon juice
1 cup sugar
2½ cups water
lemon and lime slices for garnish
maraschino cherries for garnish

Pour boiling water over tea bags and let steep for approximately 5 minutes; remove tea bags and set aside. Pour pineapple juice, apricot nectar, orange juice, lemon juice, sugar and water into the slow cooker. Set on low and cook for 1 hour. Stir in tea; taste and adjust sweetness to your personal taste. Float lemon and lime slices and a few maraschino cherries on top for garnish. Serve warm.

CRANBERRY GLOGG

This is a holiday beverage from which you can eliminate the wine to serve to children or nondrinkers.

1 qt. cranberry apple juice
2 cups Burgundy wine
¾ cup sugar
¾ cup water
1 stick (4-inch) cinnamon
3-4 cardamom pods, crushed

6 whole cloves
½ cup raisins, light and dark mixed
½ cup whole blanched almonds
peel of 1 orange, cut into strips
   for garnish

Mix cranberry apple juice, Burgundy, sugar, water, cinnamon stick, cardamom pods and cloves together; cover and chill for 8 to 12 hours. Pour mixture into the slow cooker and heat on low for about 1 hour. If desired, you can strain off spices. Add raisins and almonds. Taste and add more cranberry apple juice if too spicy. Float orange peel strips which have been tied into knots on top of mixture for garnish. When serving, be sure to ladle some raisins and almonds into each cup.

NOTE: If you desire a nonalcoholic drink, substitute 2 cups additional cranberry apple juice and eliminate Burgundy, sugar and water.

MULLED CIDER

This is a sweet, spicy mixture that is loved by all, especially children.

¾ cup packed brown sugar
1 tsp. ground cloves
1 tsp. ground allspice
1 tsp. ground cinnamon
¼ tsp. salt
1 gal. apple cider

Mix together brown sugar, cloves, allspice, cinnamon and salt. Place mixture in the slow cooker with apple cider and heat on low until sugar dissolves. Taste and if mixture is too spicy, add more apple cider.

MULLED WINE

For wine lovers, this is a must during the holidays!

1 qt. water
12 whole cloves
10 whole allspice
1 stick (6-inch) cinnamon
2 orange rinds
2 tbs. sugar
2 bottles wine, preferably claret
peel of 1 orange, cut into strips for garnish

Place water, cloves, allspice, cinnamon stick, and orange rinds (which have been left in large pieces for easy removal) in the slow cooker. Set cooker on high and allow mixture to heat almost to a boil. Add sugar and turn off slow cooker; allow mixture to steep for 45 minutes. Strain off spices and orange rinds; add wine and turn slow cooker on low. Allow mixture to heat to warm and garnish with orange peel strips which have been tied into knots.

HOT PEACH PUNCH

To offer something different during the holidays, try this spicy peach punch.

1 can (46 oz.) peach nectar
20 oz. orange juice
½ cup light brown sugar
1 stick (4-inch) cinnamon
¾ tsp. whole cloves
2 tbs. lime juice

Combine peach nectar, orange juice and brown sugar in the slow cooker. Break up cinnamon stick and mix with whole cloves. Tie spices together in a cheesecloth bag and drop into cooker. Set cooker on low and allow to heat for 1 hour before serving. Stir mixture to make sure sugar has dissolved. Add lime juice. Taste and adjust quantity of sugar or juices to your personal preference. Serve directly from slow cooker.

HOT SPIKED APPLE PUNCH

Makes: 1 gallon

We've all had hot, spiced apple cider, but dress it up with a flavored liqueur or liquor and a dollop of whipped cream and you have pizzazz!

1 gal. apple cider
2 tbs. broken cinnamon sticks
1 tbs. whole cloves
liquor or liqueur of choice — vodka, apple jack, apple liqueurs, etc.
allspice for garnish
whipped cream for garnish

Add apple cider, cinnamon sticks and cloves to the slow cooker and cook on low for 2 hours. Pour liquor into each cup and add hot spiced apple cider to fill. Sprinkle with allspice and top with a dollop of whipped cream.

GOOD OLD GROG

This grog is a mixture of port and bourbon, sweetened and spiced.

2 qt. ruby port
1½ cups dark raisins
½ cup sugar
12 whole cardamom seeds
3 sticks (4-inch each) cinnamon
1½ cups bourbon

Pour port into the slow cooker and stir in raisins and sugar. Place cardamom seeds and cinnamon sticks in a piece of cheesecloth and tie with a string. Set spice bag in port and cook on low for 2 to 3 hours. Before serving, remove spice bag and add bourbon.

HOT SPICED WINE

Servings: 6

Serve this directly from the slow cooker, leaving the orange floating for eye appeal. If you wish, add a few slices of lemon for additional garnish.

1 qt. red wine
2/3 cup sugar
1/4 cup lemon juice
1 stick (4-inch) cinnamon
1/4 tsp. nutmeg
1 whole orange
12 whole cloves

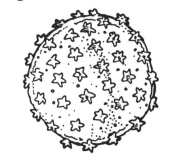

Stir wine, sugar and lemon juice into the slow cooker. Add cinnamon stick and nutmeg. Stud orange with cloves and float in cooker. Set cooker on low and allow to simmer for about 1 hour, stirring to make sure sugar has dissolved.

RUSSIAN TEA

I'm always looking for new beverages to serve at parties. This is an unusual warm punch that mixes citrus, almond and spices together.

2 cups sugar
2 cups water
2 cups orange juice
¼ cup lemon juice
½ gal. water
1 tsp. almond extract
2 tsp. vanilla extract
6 whole cloves
2 sticks (3-inch each) cinnamon

In a saucepan, boil water and sugar together for 5 minutes or until sugar dissolves completely. Pour into the slow cooker. Add remaining ingredients. Set cooker on low and cook for at least 1 hour before serving. Serve directly from slow cooker.

SOUPS

VEGETARIAN STOCK

Makes: 2 quarts

This is a great vegetable stock to use in place of chicken or beef broth in soups or sauces. It is totally fat-free! Consider using stocks instead of oil to sauté foods.

2½ qt. water
2 medium onions, chopped
3-4 stalks celery, chopped
3-4 carrots, sliced
2 potatoes, unpeeled and chopped

4 whole cloves garlic, peeled
1 bunch parsley stems
1-1½ tsp. salt
½ tsp. peppercorns
1 bay leaf

Place all ingredients in the slow cooker. Set on low and allow to cook for 10 hours. Strain off vegetables; taste remaining stock and adjust seasonings to your personal preference. Cooked vegetables can be eaten separately. Another option is to process cooked vegetables finely in a food processor or blender and add mixture back to stock for thick, colorful stock. Keep in mind that thicker stock cannot be used for replacement of basic chicken or beef stock in soup or sauce recipes.

NOTE: Parsley stems are used in place of parsley sprigs which turn stock green.

BLACK BEAN SOUP

Black beans have become very popular lately. They are healthful and have great flavor. Keep in mind that the red pepper really spices up this recipe, so you may want to be cautious about the size of the pepper or possibly eliminate it. This soup needs a little color, so I suggest using either one or several of the suggested garnishes.

2 cups dried black beans
6-8 cups chicken, beef or vegetable broth
1 large onion, chopped
4 cloves garlic, crushed
1 whole dried red serrano pepper
2 tsp. cumin
2 tsp. oregano
½ tsp. cinnamon
2 bay leaves
2 tsp. salt
2-3 carrots, sliced
3 stalks celery, sliced
sour cream, chopped tomatoes, roasted red pepper sauce, minced parsley and/or
  minced cilantro for garnish, optional

Rinse beans and place in the slow cooker. Add broth. Use 6 cups for thick soup or 8 cups for thinner soup. Stir in remaining ingredients and cover. Set on low and cook for 9 to 10 hours.

NOTE: For a higher protein meal, add a ham hock at the start of cooking period and shred meat from bone at end or add cubed, cooked ham just before serving.

SPECIAL NOTE: A product named Beano is available in health food and grocery stores which can be added to soup after cooking to help reduce gaseous effects of beans!

HUNGARIAN LAMB SOUP

Servings: 10-12

Lamb soup is a delightful change from the old standard. It is important to use a good paprika. I prefer the sweet Hungarian variety.

¼ cup butter
2 medium onions, chopped
2 lb. lamb shoulder
1 tbs. Hungarian paprika
2 qt. beef stock
2 bay leaves

salt and pepper to taste
2-3 potatoes, peeled and cubed
½ cup sliced fresh green beans
1 tbs. flour
1 cup sour cream

In a skillet, melt butter and add onions. While onions are sautéing, trim lamb of fat and cut into 1-inch cubes. Add lamb to skillet and brown. Stir in paprika and heat for 1 minute. Pour skillet ingredients into the slow cooker with stock, bay leaves, salt and pepper. Set cooker on low and cook for 6 to 7 hours. Add potatoes and green beans and cook on low for 2 to 3 hours. Half an hour before serving, mix flour with sour cream. Gently stir mixture into soup and allow to heat before serving. Taste and adjust seasonings.

TOMATO MINESTRONE

This is a quick and simple version of the traditional Italian soup. You can vary the pastas for a different texture.

2 tbs. olive oil
1 lb. beef stew meat
1 large onion, chopped
1 cup chopped celery
2 cups tomato sauce
salt and pepper to taste
1 tsp. oregano, or more to taste
2 qt. water

1½ cups sliced zucchini
1 cup frozen peas
2 cups precooked orzo pasta, or pasta
 of choice
1 tbs. chopped parsley
Parmesan or cheddar cheese sprinkles
 for garnish, optional

Heat oil in a skillet. Brown stew meat in oil. Place browned meat, onion, celery, tomato sauce, salt, pepper, oregano and water in the slow cooker. Cook on low for 6 to 8 hours. Remove meat pieces and dice meat into smaller pieces. Return meat to slow cooker; add zucchini and cook for an additional half hour or until zucchini is done. Just before serving, add peas, precooked pasta and parsley. Taste and adjust seasonings. If desired, serve with a sprinkling of Parmesan or cheddar cheese.

SPLIT PEA AND HAM SOUP

Servings: 8-10

This soup is nutritious and filling. The addition of a smoked ham shank gives it a slightly smoky flavor.

4 slices bacon, diced
1½ medium onions, chopped
2 carrots, diced
2 stalks celery, diced
1 lb. dried split peas
1 smoked ham shank

2 bay leaves
3 qt. water
¼-½ tsp. cayenne pepper
salt and pepper to taste
1 cup cooked ham, diced
croutons or fresh peas for garnish

In a skillet, fry bacon until crisp; remove and drain on paper towels. Sauté onions, carrots and celery in bacon fat for 5 minutes. Place bacon, sautéed vegetables, peas, ham shank, bay leaves, water, cayenne pepper, salt and pepper in the slow cooker. Set cooker on low and cook for 8 to 9 hours or until peas are soft. If you wish to have a smooth texture, puree soup in a food processor or blender and return to slow cooker. Add diced ham before serving and stir until heated through. Taste and adjust seasonings. Garnish with croutons or a few fresh peas.

PROVENÇAL VEGETABLE SOUP

Garlic paste makes this different from traditional vegetable soup.

1 medium onion, diced
1 leek, diced
2 cups fresh green beans
2 cups peeled, diced potatoes
2 cups diced carrots
2 cups diced tomatoes
2½ qt. water
salt and pepper to taste
2 zucchini, diced
½ lb. mushrooms, sliced

3 cloves garlic
2 tbs. chopped fresh basil or 2 tsp.
 dried basil
dash salt
1 can (6 oz.) tomato paste
¼ cup grated Parmesan cheese
¼ cup olive oil
grated Parmesan cheese or chopped
 parsley for garnish

In the slow cooker, place onion, leek, green beans, potatoes, carrots, tomatoes and water. Cook on low for 8 hours. Add salt, pepper, zucchini and mushrooms and cook 1 hour longer. With a mortar and pestle or a wooden spoon, crush garlic and mix in chopped basil and salt until a paste is formed. To this paste, add tomato paste, Parmesan cheese and olive oil and mix well. Add a bit of soup to paste; then stir paste into soup. Blend well and allow to heat for 15 minutes before serving. Taste and adjust seasonings. Garnish with Parmesan cheese or parsley.

CREAM OF CHESTNUT SOUP

This is a delicious, unique soup, perfect for the holidays, especially as a starter course for an elegant roast goose dinner. If fresh chestnuts are not readily available, use canned chestnuts. I like to garnish this soup with homemade croutons.

2 lb. fresh chestnuts, skinned
4 cups chicken stock
½ cup butter
2 medium onions, chopped
6 stalks celery, diced
salt and pepper to taste
2 tbs. butter
1 tbs. flour
1 cup light cream

Place chestnuts in the slow cooker and cover with stock and ¼ cup butter. Set on low and cook for 3 to 4 hours or until chestnuts are soft. Strain off chestnuts; reserve liquid and puree softened chestnuts in a food processor or blender until smooth. Add a little liquid, if needed, to make mixture smooth. In a heavy saucepan, melt remaining butter and add onions. Cover and cook until soft but not brown. Stir in chestnut puree and add remaining stock and celery. Season to taste with salt and pepper. Blend butter and flour together and add to soup, stirring until thickened. Strain soup; add cream and heat just to a boil. Retaste for seasoning. Serve with croutons.

CROUTONS

4 slices bread
2 tbs. oil
$\frac{1}{4}$ cup butter
salt, optional

Slice bread into small cubes. Heat oil and butter in a skillet on medium high and toss in cubed bread. Stir bread constantly, turning heat down if bread begins to darken too quickly. Toss on heat until bread cubes are nicely browned. Drain on absorbent paper and sprinkle with salt (this helps to reduce the oily flavor).

BEST EVER CHICKEN STOCK

Makes: 1 gallon

Chicken stock is the basis for many soups and sauces, and can be used in place of butter or oil to add flavor without fat when frying vegetables. Adding onion skins to the stock will give it extra flavor and a darker color.

2 lb. chicken parts
1 lb. veal bones
1 gal. cold water
4 carrots, diced
2 medium onions, diced
½ tsp. whole cloves
3 stalks celery, diced
1 tbs. salt

1 tsp. black peppercorns
handful parsley stems, not leaves
2 bay leaves
1 rosemary sprig or 1 tsp. dried
1 thyme sprig or 1 tsp. dried
few blades mace, or dash nutmeg
2 whole cloves garlic, peeled

Place chicken parts and veal bones in the slow cooker and cover with water. Turn slow cooker on high and as scum rises to top, remove it with a slotted spoon. After scum ceases to form, turn slow cooker on low and add remaining ingredients. If fresh rosemary and thyme are not available, wrap dried rosemary and thyme in cheesecloth; place in pot and remove at end of cooking. Cook for 6 hours; strain broth; taste and adjust seasonings. When cool, refrigerate until ready to use.

CREAM OF CHICKEN SOUP

Once you have a great stock, you can quickly make a cream of chicken soup. If you wish, pour a little cream into the center of each serving.

4 cups chicken stock
2 cups chopped celery
2 cloves garlic, minced
3/4 cup half-and-half
salt and white pepper to taste
2 cups minced precooked chicken
1/2 cup grated Parmesan cheese

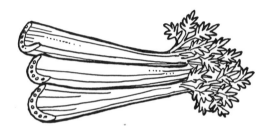

Put stock, celery and garlic in the slow cooker. Set on high and cook until celery is tender, about 30 minutes. Pour mixture into a food processor or blender and puree until smooth. Return pureed mixture to pot and turn cooker on low. Add remaining ingredients and stir until heated through and cheese has melted.

SPANISH PORK AND BEAN SOUP

Servings: 10-12

This is definitely a main course soup — hearty with beans, Spanish sausage and smoked ham. I like to serve it with a tossed salad and corn bread or tortillas.

¼ lb. dried chickpeas
¼ lb. dried navy beans
¼ lb. salt pork or bacon, diced
¼ lb. Spanish sausage (chorizo) or
  garlic sausage
¼ lb. smoked ham, diced
2 qt. beef stock
3 cloves garlic, minced

1 ham bone
2 tomatoes, chopped
1½ tsp. cumin
4-5 potatoes, peeled, diced
salt and pepper to taste
½ lb. fresh spinach
3 tbs. butter

Rinse chickpeas and navy beans; cover with water and soak overnight. Drain and discard water. In a skillet, fry salt pork until browned. Remove pork and fry sausage until thoroughly cooked. Discard fat. Cut sausage into slices and set aside with salt pork and ham. Place peas and beans in the slow cooker with stock, garlic, ham bone, tomatoes, cumin, potatoes, salt and pepper. Cook on low for 8 to 9 hours or until chickpeas are tender. Wash spinach well and sauté in butter in skillet until all liquid is evaporated. Add cooked spinach and reserved meats to soup. Taste and adjust seasonings. If desired, garnish with *Croutons,* page 47.

BEEF VEGETABLE BARLEY SOUP

Servings: 10-12

This is an easy recipe with a secret ingredient, oatmeal, that gives it body and a special flavor.

1 lb. beef stew meat, cut into 1-inch
  cubes
1 large beef knuckle bone, cut in half
1 large onion, diced
3 stalks celery, coarsely chopped
2 whole cloves garlic, peeled
1 tsp. salt
1 medium rutabaga, peeled, cut into
  1/2-inch cubes

3 qt. water
8 carrots, cut into 1-inch pieces
2 parsnips, peeled, cut into 1/2-inch
  pieces
3 beef bouillon cubes
1 cup barley
1/2 cup oatmeal
salt and pepper to taste

Place stew meat, knuckle bone, onion, celery, garlic, salt, rutabaga and water in the slow cooker. Set on low and cook for 7 to 8 hours. Remove knuckle bone and strip off any meat and marrow. Discard bone. Add meat and marrow to slow cooker. Add carrots, parsnips and bouillon cubes and cook on low for 2 hours. Add barley and oatmeal and cook for 1 to 2 hours. Taste and add salt and pepper, if desired. Soup is done when vegetables are tender.

CHICKPEA SOUP

Servings: 10-12

This is a hearty soup made from chickpeas, sausage, cabbage and a pinch of saffron.

1 lb. dried chickpeas
3 qt. chicken or beef stock
1 ham bone
pinch saffron
2-3 bay leaves
4 cloves garlic, minced
2 medium onions, chopped
2 cups potatoes, peeled, diced
1-2 cooked Spanish sausage (chorizo), sliced
3 cups cabbage, finely chopped
salt and pepper to taste

Soak chickpeas in water overnight; drain and discard water. Place chickpeas in the slow cooker with stock, ham bone, saffron, bay leaves, garlic and onions. Set cooker on low and cook for 8 hours. Add potatoes, sausage, cabbage, salt and pepper and cook for 2 hours longer or until potatoes are done. Remove ham bone; cut off any meat from bone; discard bone and add ham back to pot. Taste and adjust seasonings.

VICHYSSOISE

This is a classic leek and potato soup that has been adapted to the slow cooker. Traditionally this soup is served cold but it can be served hot.

2 lb. leeks
2 lb. potatoes
7 cups chicken stock
2¼ cups milk

1½ cups cream
salt and white pepper to taste
fresh chopped chives for garnish

Trim off tough green leaves from leeks; split bulbs open and carefully wash out dirt between layers. Thinly slice leeks. Peel potatoes and dice. Place leeks, potatoes and chicken stock in the slow cooker; set on low and cook for 3 to 4 hours or until vegetables are tender. Puree entire mixture in a food processor or blender. Return mixture to slow cooker and add milk, cream, salt and white pepper. Cook on low until mixture is heated through. Taste and adjust seasoning. If serving chilled, allow soup to come to room temperature and then refrigerate. Garnish with fresh chopped chives.

LENTIL SOUP

Lentils are high in protein and full of fiber. I think this soup is better the second day. If served with a side dish of rice, you have a meal of complete protein.

2 tbs. butter
½-¾ cup onion, diced
2-3 cloves garlic, minced
1½ cups dried lentils
4 cups water
2 cups tomato juice
1 tsp. salt, or more to taste
2 bay leaves
pinch dill seed, optional

Turn the slow cooker on high and melt butter in pot. Add onion and garlic and sauté until tender. Turn cooker on low. Rinse lentils well and drain. Add lentils and water to cooker and cook on low for 4 to 5 hours. Add tomato juice, salt, bay leaves and dill seed, if desired, and cook an additional 3 hours. Taste and adjust seasonings.

LAMB AND BEAN SOUP

This is a delicious, hearty soup.

¾ cup dried white beans
¾ cup dried kidney beans
2 lb. lamb shanks
2 medium onions, sliced
3 leeks, sliced
1 turnip, peeled and diced
½ cup shredded cabbage
3 tomatoes, peeled, seeded and
  coarsely chopped
1 cup chopped green and
  red bell peppers, mixed

½ cup sliced mushrooms
3 tbs. finely chopped celery
6 cloves garlic, minced
3 bay leaves
1 tsp. summer savory
1 tsp. salt, or to taste
¼ tsp. pepper
1 cup red wine
2½ qt. water
chopped parsley and grated Parmesan
  cheese for garnish

Into the slow cooker, place white and kidney beans; cover with water and let soak overnight. Drain and discard water. Add remaining ingredients except garnish. Set cooker on low for 10 to 12 hours. Occasionally skim off fat that forms on surface. Remove bay leaves and lamb shanks. Strip any remaining meat from bones; discard bones and add meat back to slow cooker. Taste and adjust seasonings. Garnish.

VEGETARIAN ENTRÉES

FALAFEL (CHICKPEA BURGERS)

Servings: 6

Falafel is a Middle Eastern vegetarian dish made from garbanzo beans which are formed into little patties and quickly fried. They are good served in pita bread with hummus and either sprouts or tabbouleh salad. Traditionally, this is served with tahini (sesame paste) dip.

½ lb. dried garbanzo beans or
  fava beans
water to cover
1 tbs. chopped cilantro
1 tbs. chopped parsley
4 green onions, chopped

2 cloves garlic, minced
½-1 tsp. cumin
pinch baking soda
salt and pepper to taste
water to moisten, optional
olive oil for frying

Rinse dried beans under running water; place in the slow cooker and cover with water (at least 2 inches over top of beans). Cook on low for 8 to 10 hours. Pour off water; rinse under cold water and allow to drain. Place cooked beans in a food processor or blender and puree until slightly grainy. Add cilantro, parsley, onions, garlic, cumin, soda, salt and pepper. Blend until just mixed. Taste mixture and adjust seasonings. Moisten your hands with water and form mixture into small patties. If mixture seems too dry to form proper patties, add a small amount of water. Heat olive oil in a skillet and fry patties until brown on both sides.

KAMUT VEGETABLE SALAD

Servings: 6-8

This healthy, chewy grain complements vegetables perfectly.

1 cup whole grain kamut
3 cups water
½ tsp. salt
1 cup chopped celery
1 cup chopped red cabbage

½ cup diced red bell peppers
¼ cup diced green onions
¼ cup diced red onion
2-4 tbs. chopped cilantro, to taste

Place kamut, water and salt in the slow cooker. Set on low and cook 8 to 9 hours. Allow grains to cool thoroughly. Mix in celery, cabbage, peppers, red and green onions and cilantro. Make vinaigrette recipe and add enough vinaigrette to moisten.

BALSAMIC VINAIGRETTE

1 cup olive oil
⅓ cup balsamic vinegar
1 tsp. Dijon mustard

1-2 tsp. sugar
salt and pepper to taste

Mix all ingredients together in a food processor or blender. Taste and add additional seasonings to your personal taste.

MARINATED GARBANZO BEAN SALAD

Servings: 6

Instead of the same old three-bean salad, try something new. This salad can be served warm or cold.

3 cups dried garbanzo beans
water to cover
1 tbs. olive oil
2 tbs. vegetable stock or chicken stock
1/2 cup chopped onion

1 tbs. thyme
1/2 red bell pepper, chopped
1/2 cup currants or raisins
2 tbs. balsamic vinegar

In the slow cooker, cover dried beans with water (at least 2 inches above beans). Cook on low for 8 hours. Drain beans; discard water and measure out 3 cups. (If there are extra beans, add to a tossed salad or use to make hummus dip.) Place oil and 1 tbs. vegetable stock in a skillet. Add onion and thyme; cook on medium until onion is soft and beginning to turn brown, about 10 minutes. Add remaining 1 tbs. vegetable stock and pepper; stir-fry for several minutes. Add currants and cooked beans; cook for 5 minutes. Remove mixture from heat, pour into a bowl and let cool. Add vinegar and mix well. Taste and add more seasonings or vinegar to taste.

LAYERED BLACK BEAN SALAD

Servings: 6-8

A colorful, unique salad, this goes well with com chips or a crusty bread.

BEAN MIXTURE

1 cup dried black beans
4 cups water
½ cup chopped green bell peppers
½ cup chopped red bell peppers

½ cup chopped yellow bell peppers
½ cup chopped onion
dash red pepper flakes

Rinse dried beans and place in the slow cooker. Cover with water; set cooker on low and cook for 8 to 9 hours. Remove beans from cooker; discard water and rinse beans. Allow to cool. Mix beans with peppers, onion and pepper flakes; set aside.

DRESSING

1 cup balsamic red wine vinegar
¾ cup olive oil
2-3 cloves garlic, peeled

1 tbs. sugar
salt to taste

Mix vinegar, olive oil, whole garlic cloves, sugar and salt in a saucepan. Simmer for 10 minutes. Cool and strain. Pour cooled dressing over bean mixture and allow flavors to blend for at least 2 hours or overnight, if time permits.

SALAD INGREDIENTS

sour cream, low fat if available
bottled salsa
chopped lettuce
chopped green onions
chopped parsley for garnish

Because size of the bowl determines quantity of salad ingredients, exact measurements cannot be determined. I like to serve this in a straight-sided glass bowl. Place half of bean mixture in bottom of bowl. Spread a thin layer of sour cream over beans and then a thin layer of salsa. Follow with a 1 inch-thick layer of chopped lettuce; sprinkle with chopped green onions and top with remaining bean mixture. Sprinkle with chopped parsley.

BLACK BEAN CHILI

This is ideal for cold, autumn or winter days. Black beans add great flavor and are low fat. If served with rice or potatoes, this makes a healthy, complete protein meal.

1 cup dried black beans
4 cups water
½ tsp. cumin seeds
⅛ tsp. cayenne pepper
½ tsp. paprika
1 medium onion, chopped
3 cloves garlic, mashed
1 tsp. dry mustard
1 tsp. chili powder
2 large tomatoes, preferably plum variety
2 tbs. tomato paste
½ red bell pepper, chopped
1 can (4 oz.) diced green chilies
6 oz. low fat cheese, shredded
salt to taste

Soak beans in water overnight. Drain and discard water. Place beans and water in the slow cooker and set on high. Cook until tender, about 6 hours. The next step is not necessary, but I find that it really intensifies the flavor. Heat a skillet on medium and toast cumin seeds until they begin to pop, about 2 to 3 minutes. Add cayenne pepper and paprika and cook for 1 minute. (**Note**: This is very volatile so have the fan running.) To cooked beans in slow cooker, add toasted spices and onion. Mix mashed garlic with dry mustard and add to bean mixture. Add chili powder. Seed and chop tomatoes and add to pot with tomato paste, pepper and green chilies. Set cooker on low and allow to cook for 3 to 4 hours. Before serving, add shredded cheese. Taste and add salt, if desired.

ALTERNATIVES: To make a dip or to use as a sandwich spread, omit the cheese and puree mixture in a food processor or blender.

SIMPLE TOMATO SAUCE

Try this recipe for a quick, tasty sauce that takes just minutes to prepare. Serve over pasta or spaghetti squash with a sprinkling of Parmesan for a good vegetarian meal.

2 tbs. olive oil
1 large onion, chopped
4-5 cups canned plum tomatoes, undrained
1 can (6 oz.) tomato paste
2 tsp. basil
2 tsp. oregano
2 tsp. sugar
salt and pepper to taste
1 cup fresh mushrooms, sliced, optional

Turn the slow cooker on high; add oil and onion. Allow onion to soften and wilt slightly. Set cooker on low, add remaining ingredients and cook for 4 to 6 hours. Taste and season to your personal preference before serving.

LENTIL SPAGHETTI SAUCE

Servings: 6

Spaghetti sauce is generally loved by all, but if you want to cut down on fat and meats, lentils are a good substitute.

1 tbs. olive oil
1 medium onion, chopped
2-3 cloves garlic, minced
2 cans (15 oz. each) tomato sauce
1 cup chopped fresh tomato
1 cup water
1/2 cup lentils

1/2 tsp. oregano
1 tsp. basil
1/2 tsp. salt
1/2 tsp. thyme
dash red pepper flakes, cayenne
    pepper or Tabasco Sauce, optional

Set the slow cooker on high. Add oil and when hot, sauté onion and garlic until wilted. Turn cooker to low; add tomato sauce, fresh tomato and water. Wash lentils well and add to slow cooker with remaining ingredients. Cook for 6 to 7 hours. Serve over pasta, cooked, shredded spaghetti squash or rice.

MEAT ENTRÉES

MEXICAN POT ROAST

Add a little flare to your standard pot roast by cooking it in a tomato-based sauce rich with garlic.

2 tbs. olive oil
4-5 lb. beef pot roast
salt and pepper to taste
1 medium onion, chopped
3 cloves garlic, minced

1 can (16 oz.) chopped tomatoes
2 bay leaves
½ tsp. thyme
1 cup fresh sliced mushrooms or
    canned mushrooms, optional

Heat olive oil in a skillet. Sprinkle roast with salt and pepper and brown well on all sides. Remove from skillet and set aside. Place remaining ingredients in the slow cooker and stir. Add browned roast; set cooker on low and cook for 8 to 10 hours. Roast is done when meat is tender enough to be cut with a fork.

NOTE: For a unique flavor, you may add 1 cup of white wine at the beginning of cooking cycle.

CABBAGE ROLLS AND SAUERKRAUT

This is a fantastic recipe for cabbage rolls with a slightly sweet-and-sour, tomato-based sauce.

1 large cabbage
1 small onion, chopped
1 lb. lean ground beef
2 cloves garlic, minced
1 cup cooked rice
1 tbs. salt
½ tsp. pepper
¾ tsp. thyme
½ tsp. paprika
1 jar (22 oz.) sauerkraut
1 jar (1 lb.) chopped tomatoes
3 tbs. lemon juice
3 tbs. brown sugar
¼ cup vermouth
2 bay leaves
sour cream for garnish, optional

Remove cabbage core with a sharp knife. Parboil cabbage, core cavity side down, for approximately 5 minutes to slightly wilt leaves and make them more pliable. Carefully separate leaves and cut out thickest part of stems with a small V-cut to make leaves easier to wrap.

Mix onion, beef, garlic, rice, salt, pepper, thyme and paprika together in a bowl until well combined. Pour undrained sauerkraut into the slow cooker. Cup 1 cabbage leaf in your hand and fill with several tablespoons of meat mixture. Wrap leaf around meat mixture; fold in all 4 sides and secure with a wooden toothpick. Place on sauerkraut, seam side down. Repeat until all meat mixture is used. Mix together undrained tomatoes, lemon juice, brown sugar and vermouth; pour over cabbage rolls. Tuck bay leaves in juice where they can be easily removed later. Set cooker on low and cook for 10 to 12 hours. Serve cabbage rolls with sauce on top and a little sauerkraut. If desired, top with a dollop of sour cream.

BEER STEW

This is a basic beef stew with a twist — beer. It adds a unique flavor and helps tenderize the meat.

2½ lb. beef stew meat, clod roast or
  chuck roast
1 large onion, chopped
2 cloves garlic, minced
4-5 carrots, cut into chunks
2-3 stalks celery, cut into slices
16 oz. beer

2½ tsp. salt
½ tsp. pepper
1½ tsp. oregano
2 tbs. tomato paste
3-4 tbs. melted butter
⅓ cup flour
chopped parsley for garnish, optional

Cut beef into 1-inch squares. Place beef, onion, garlic, carrots, celery, beer, salt, pepper, oregano and tomato paste in the slow cooker. Set cooker on low and cook for 8 to 10 hours. Mix melted butter with flour until a smooth, thick paste is formed and stir into stew. Taste stew and adjust seasonings to your personal preference. Turn slow cooker on high and allow mixture to thicken before serving. Garnish with chopped parsley.

NOTE: If you like potatoes in your stew, add canned potatoes (cut into chunks) just before serving.

SPECIAL BOLOGNESE SAUCE

My friend, Sam, brought me a sample of a sauce he had obtained in his travels and asked me to try to duplicate it. The secret ingredients that made this sauce unique were thyme and Dijon mustard, which, I'm sure, aren't normal Italian flavors! Give it a try — you might be pleasantly surprised.

1½ lb. lean ground beef
1 cup chopped onion
2 carrots, chopped
2 stalks celery, chopped
5 cups chopped, canned tomatoes
1 cup white wine
1½ tsp. salt
½ tsp. pepper

4 cloves garlic, minced
2 tsp. oregano
2 tsp. basil
1 tsp. rosemary
½ tsp. anise seeds
1 tbs. thyme
1½ tbs. Dijon mustard
1 tbs. sugar, or to taste

In a skillet, brown beef and onion until no red remains in meat and beef is crumbled. Drain off excess fat. Place browned beef and onion in the slow cooker and stir in remaining ingredients. Cover and set cooker on low for 6 to 8 hours. Taste and adjust seasonings. Serve over hot pasta.

SOUTH AMERICAN BRAISED BEEF

Servings: 4

Slow cooking can turn even a round steak into a cut-with-a-fork tender piece of meat. I usually shred the meat and, with a little sauce, use it to fill tortillas.

2 cloves garlic, minced
2 lb. beef round steak
1 tsp. salt
¼ tsp. pepper
2 tbs. lime or lemon juice
1 medium onion, chopped
1 cup chopped carrots
1 tsp. marjoram
½ cup beef broth
1 can (14½ oz.) peeled tomatoes

Spread minced garlic on round steak and sprinkle with salt, pepper and lime juice. Place in the slow cooker and add remaining ingredients. Set cooker on low and cook for approximately 8 hours. Meat should be fork tender and shred easily. If not, return to pot and cook additional time. Taste and add extra seasonings if desired.

PICADILLO

Picadillo is a spicy, pickled-type meat mixture that is very popular in Mexico. It can be used in burritos, tacos, turnovers, empanadas or even stuffed in chiles rellenos.

3 lb. boneless pork
½ large onion, sliced
3 cloves garlic, peeled and left whole
1 tbs. salt
water to cover meat
¼ cup butter
½ large onion, finely chopped
3 cloves garlic, minced

8 peppercorns
5 whole cloves
½-inch stick cinnamon
¼ cup raisins
2 tbs. slivered almonds
2-3 tbs. chopped candied fruit
2 tsp. salt, or to taste
1½ lb. tomatoes, peeled and seeded

Cut meat into large cubes and place in the slow cooker. Add onion, garlic and salt. Cover mixture with water and cook on low for 8 to 10 hours. Strain meat; allow to cool and shred or cut into small cubes. Heat butter in a skillet and sauté onion and minced garlic on medium until soft but not brown. Add meat and cook until it begins to brown. Crush peppercorns, cloves and cinnamon with a mortar and pestle or electric seed grinder and add to meat mixture. Gently stir in remaining ingredients except tomatoes. Mash tomatoes slightly and add to meat mixture. Cook on high in skillet, stirring occasionally until moisture in mixture is evaporated. Taste and adjust seasonings.

COLORADO CHILI

This chili is made with large red (Colorado) chili peppers which are ground into a paste and added to cooked meat. Beans make a great accompaniment.

2 lb. lean beef or pork
2 cups water
salt to taste
8 large dried red Colorado chili peppers
warm water to cover chili peppers
2 cloves garlic, peeled

1 tsp. oregano
¼ cup oil, or less if desired
2 tbs. flour
salt to taste
pinch cumin, or to taste

Cut beef or pork into cubes and place in the slow cooker with water and salt. Cook on high for 1 to 2 hours. Drain meat and reserve liquid. While meat is cooking, cover peppers with warm water and allow to soak for 20 to 30 minutes. Drain peppers and reserve liquid. Cut peppers open and remove seeds. Puree peppers, garlic and oregano in a food processor or blender to consistency of paste. To paste, add 1 cup reserved meat liquid and ½ cup reserved liquid from chili peppers. Stir until well mixed. In a skillet, heat oil; stir in flour and add chili mixture, salt and cumin. Add chili mixture to slow cooker with meat and set on low. Cook for 4 to 6 hours. Taste and adjust seasonings.

OLIVE SPAGHETTI SAUCE

When the "old red spaghetti sauce" gets boring, try something new. This sauce is made with green olives, but, if you don't like them, you can substitute black olives.

1 lb. lean ground beef
½ lb. ground veal
¼ lb. Italian sausage
1 cup water
1 tsp. salt
⅛ tsp. pepper
1 can (28 oz.) tomatoes, chopped
12 oz. tomato paste
1½ cups Burgundy wine
1 cup chopped onion

¾ cup chopped green bell pepper
3 cloves garlic, crushed
2 tsp. sugar
½ tsp. chili powder
1½ tsp. Worcestershire sauce
3 bay leaves
1 cup sliced mushrooms, fresh or canned
½ cup sliced stuffed green olives
grated Parmesan cheese

In a heavy skillet, brown beef, veal and sausage. Drain off fat. Put browned meat, water, salt, pepper, tomatoes, tomato paste, Burgundy, onion, peppers, garlic, sugar, chili powder, Worcestershire sauce, bay leaves and fresh mushrooms (not canned) in the slow cooker. Cook on low for 8 hours. About half an hour before serving, add olives to cooker. Add canned mushrooms if you are using them. Cook half an hour longer. Serve over pasta and sprinkle with Parmesan.

INCREDIBLE CHILI

Servings: 12

This is the "true" chili made the old-fashioned way. It's worth the effort.

½ lb. bacon, diced
3 medium onions, minced
1½ lb. pork loin
1½ lb. sirloin tip
1½ lb. ground chuck (chili grind)
2 cans (15 oz. each) tomato sauce
18 oz. beer
3 cloves garlic, minced

1 jalapeño pepper, seeded and minced
2 tbs. ground cumin
½ tsp. oregano
2-3 tbs. mild chili powder
salt and pepper to taste
2 cups dried pinto beans, optional
grated cheese, optional

In a skillet, fry bacon until brown. Drain and place in the slow cooker. Remove all but a small amount of fat from skillet and sauté onions until slightly brown. Place onions in slow cooker. Cut pork loin and sirloin tip into ¼-inch dice and brown with ground chuck in skillet. Drain off fat and add meat to slow cooker. Add remaining ingredients except cheese. If you choose to use pinto beans, soak in water overnight, discard water, add beans to slow cooker and stir. Set cooker on low and cook for 6 to 8 hours. Meat should be very tender. Taste and adjust seasonings. If desired, sprinkle with cheese before serving.

SURPRISE SPARERIBS

The ribs are cooked slowly, marinated and finally barbecued or broiled. The surprise ingredient, Coca Cola, is added to the final basting sauce.

6 lb. pork spareribs
water to cover meat
4 tsp. pickling spices
1 tsp. salt

1-1¼ cups brown sugar
2 tbs. dry mustard
½ cup ketchup
½ cup Coca Cola

Cut ribs apart and place in the slow cooker. Cover ribs with water. Add pickling spices and salt. Cook on low for 6 hours or until ribs are tender. Discard liquid and place ribs in a shallow pan. Mix brown sugar and dry mustard together and sprinkle over ribs. Cover and refrigerate overnight. Mix ketchup and Coca Cola together and spread on ribs. Grill or broil until ribs are browned.

COUNTRY RIBS

Servings: 6

I believe what makes ribs really good is tender, succulent, drop-off-the-bone meat smothered in a delicious sauce. This is the basic recipe for the ribs and several sauces — barbecue, sauerkraut and Hawaiian — that complement the meat.

4-6 lb. country-style pork or beef ribs
water to cover meat
1 large onion, chopped
3 bay leaves
1 tbs. salt
1 tsp. peppercorns
2 tbs. cider vinegar
1 cup chopped celery

Place ribs in the slow cooker and cover with water. Add remaining ingredients. Set cooker on low and cook for 8 to 12 hours, depending on size of rib and type of meat used. Meat should be very tender. Skim off top of broth and remove meat. Smother cooked meat in sauce of choice and place under a broiler to brown or on a barbecue.

BARBECUE SAUCE

¼ cup butter
2 large onions, chopped
12 oz. tomato paste
3 cloves garlic, minced
¼ cup Worcestershire sauce
¼ cup cider vinegar

½ cup brown sugar
½ cup sweet pickle relish
½ cup red or white wine
2 tsp. salt
2 tsp. dry mustard
few drops Liquid Smoke, optional

Heat butter in a heavy saucepan and sauté onions until tender. Add remaining ingredients. If you like a smoke-flavored barbecue sauce, carefully add a few drops of Liquid Smoke. Allow mixture to cook on low for about half an hour. Taste and adjust seasonings.

KRAUT AND RIBS

1 jar (32 oz.) sauerkraut
1 tsp. caraway seeds

pepper to taste, optional
chopped parsley for garnish

Heat sauerkraut, caraway seeds and pepper in a saucepan until hot. Place ribs on a platter and cover with flavored sauerkraut. Sprinkle with parsley and serve.

HAWAIIAN RIBS

½ cup brown sugar
½ cup cider vinegar
1 tsp. Worcestershire sauce
¼ cup bottled chili sauce
2 tbs. soy sauce
⅔ cup ketchup
2 cups pineapple tidbits or crushed pineapple
¼ cup cornstarch

Place sugar, vinegar, Worcestershire sauce, chili sauce, soy sauce and ketchup in a heavy saucepan and heat on medium. Drain pineapple and reserve ¼ cup of juice to mix with cornstarch. Mix juice and cornstarch together to form a paste and immediately add to heated mixture. Stir until thickened. Add drained pineapple. Taste and adjust seasonings.

BURGUNDY BEEF

Whenever you cook with wine, use a wine you would gladly drink. Don't waste the recipe with cheap wine. Use a good Burgundy in this recipe and you'll reap the rewards. Serve this with gnocchi, noodles, rice or potatoes.

4 tbs. butter
4 tbs. olive oil
1 can (1¼ lb.) small white onions
4 lb. chuck, cut into 2-inch cubes
¼ cup flour
1 tsp. Kitchen Bouquet
1 tbs. tomato paste
3 cups Burgundy wine

¼ tsp. pepper
3 bay leaves
½ tsp. thyme
½ tsp. marjoram
1 tbs. chopped fresh parsley
¾ lb. fresh or canned mushrooms
chopped fresh parsley for garnish

In a skillet, heat butter and oil; sauté onions until brown. Remove from skillet and place in the slow cooker. In same skillet, brown meat cubes on all sides; add to slow cooker. Discard all but 1 tbs. fat from skillet. Add flour, Kitchen Bouquet and tomato paste to skillet; stir until smooth. Gradually stir in Burgundy wine. Add mixture to slow cooker with pepper, bay leaves, thyme, marjoram, parsley and mushrooms. Set cooker on low and cook 8 to 9 hours. Taste and add salt, if desired. Garnish with a sprinkling of parsley.

BEEF IN BEER

This is a simple-to-fix onion and beef stew that goes well with mashed potatoes, noodles or rice.

3 lb. boneless beef chuck
2 tbs. flour
1½ tsp. salt
⅛ tsp. pepper
½ tsp. crushed rosemary
2 tbs. oil
4 medium onions, sliced into rounds

2 cloves garlic, minced
2 bay leaves
4 whole cloves
1 can (12 oz.) beer
2 tbs. red wine vinegar
1 tsp. Dijon mustard
chopped parsley for garnish

Trim fat from beef and cut into 1-inch cubes. Mix flour, salt, pepper and rosemary together and coat beef cubes. In a skillet, fry beef in oil until brown on all sides. Place beef in the slow cooker; cover with onions, garlic, bay leaves, cloves and beer. Cook on low for 8 to 9 hours or until beef is very tender. Before serving, stir in vinegar and mustard. Taste and adjust seasonings. Sprinkle with finely chopped parsley and serve.

SWEET-AND-SOUR BEEF

Sweet-and-sour is a popular flavor usually reserved for pork or chicken. This is a delicious beef version that is good served over rice or noodles.

2 lb. boneless chuck
1/3 cup flour
1 tsp. salt
1/4 tsp. black pepper
1 tbs. butter
1 tbs. olive oil
1 large onion, chopped
1/2 cup ketchup

1/4 cup brown sugar
1/4 cup red wine vinegar
1 tbs. Worcestershire sauce
1 cup water
1 tsp. salt
pepper to taste, optional
4-6 carrots, julienned

Cut beef into 1-inch cubes. Mix together flour, salt and pepper and dredge cubes in mixture. In a skillet, heat butter and olive oil and brown beef cubes. Place browned beef in the slow cooker and set on low. Add remaining ingredients except carrots. Cook for 8 to 9 hours or until meat is tender. Add carrots and cook 1 1/2 to 2 hours longer. Taste, adjust seasonings and serve.

GROUND LAMB AND ONION CURRY

Servings: 4

This is a great dish to have when you crave something spicy and different. If ground lamb is not available, you can substitute ground beef.

3 tbs. oil
2 large onions, thinly sliced
1 tbs. peeled, chopped fresh ginger
2 cloves garlic, minced
1 tsp. salt
1 lb. ground lamb
2-3 tsp. curry powder
1/4 tsp. cinnamon
1/2 tsp. turmeric

1/2 tsp. coriander powder
1/2 tsp. cumin
dash Tabasco Sauce or red pepper flakes
pepper to taste
4 cups tomatoes, peeled, seeded and chopped
2 tbs. plain yogurt
chopped cilantro for garnish

Heat oil in a skillet and add onions, ginger, garlic and salt. Sauté until onions begin to brown. Add lamb and cook until no longer pink. Drain grease from meat mixture. Add curry powder, cinnamon, turmeric, coriander, cumin, Tabasco and pepper. Stir for several minutes to release flavor of spices. Transfer ingredients to the slow cooker and set temperature to low for 1 to 2 hours. Add tomatoes and yogurt to lamb mixture and cook half an hour longer. Taste and adjust seasonings. Serve over rice and garnish liberally with chopped cilantro.

SAUSAGE AND BAKED BEANS

Even though this recipe uses canned beans, adding delicious ingredients and cooking on low for a long time really enhances the flavor.

1 lb. ground pork sausage
4-5 slices bacon, diced
1 large onion, chopped
1 stalk celery, chopped
1 can (28 oz.) baked beans
¾ tsp. basil
1 tbs. chopped parsley

2 tbs. chutney
2 tbs. soy sauce
2 tbs. cider or red wine vinegar
1 can (15 oz.) tomatoes
1 tsp. salt
½ cup molasses

Brown sausage and bacon in a skillet and drain off fat. Place browned meats in the slow cooker with remaining ingredients. Set cooker on low and cook for 6 hours. Check the quantity of liquid; if it seems excessive, pour a little off and reserve for later. Stir and continue cooking an additional 6 hours. Check to determine if you need to add some reserved liquid. Taste and adjust seasonings.

ORANGE MADEIRA POT ROAST

Servings: 6

This pot roast is marinated in a spicy, orange sauce, cooked with the marinade and finished with a thickened sauce in which Madeira is added. Serve with rice or mashed potatoes.

1 can (6 oz.) frozen orange juice
  concentrate
½ cup orange juice
1 tbs. grated orange peel
2 small onions, chopped
1½ tsp. salt
½ tsp. pepper
½ tsp. ground cloves
1¼ tsp. ground coriander

¼ tsp. cumin
3½ lb. chuck roast
1 tbs. olive oil
1 tbs. butter
2 tbs. cornstarch
¼ cup water
2 oranges, sliced
½ cup Madeira wine
chopped parsley for garnish, optional

In a bowl, mix together undiluted orange juice concentrate, orange juice, orange peel, onions, salt, pepper, cloves, coriander and cumin. Pour mixture over chuck roast and allow to marinate at least 6 hours in the refrigerator. Remove meat from marinade; scrape off excess liquid and reserve.

Heat oil and butter in a skillet on high and brown meat on both sides. Transfer meat to the slow cooker and pour reserved marinade on top. Set cooker on low for 8 to 10 hours or until tender. Remove meat to a platter and keep warm until sauce is ready.

Mix cornstarch with water and pour into slow cooker. Stir and allow to thicken. Add orange slices and Madeira and simmer for 15 minutes. Taste and adjust seasonings. Slice meat; remove orange slices from pot and arrange around meat. Pour sauce over meat. If desired, garnish with a sprinkling of chopped parsley.

WINE STEW

Stew does not have to be limited to carrots and potatoes in gravy. Try something new — mixing meats, using wine and serving with rice.

2½ lb. top sirloin
2 tbs. butter or bacon fat
½ lb. ham, preferably Westphalian
2 large onions, diced
½ cup stuffed green olives, halved
2-3 cloves garlic, minced
¾ tsp. thyme
½ cup raisins

3 cups red wine
2 tsp. pepper
1 tsp. salt, or to taste
¼ cup brandy
¾ cup cream
¼ cup flour
½ cup water

Cut sirloin into 2-inch pieces. In a skillet, heat butter on high and brown beef cubes. Add ham and onions; stir until slightly brown. Transfer mixture to the slow cooker and set on low. Add olives, garlic, thyme, raisins and wine. Cook for 7 to 8 hours. Add pepper, salt, brandy and cream; cook 1 hour longer. Remove meat from cooker and keep warm. Turn cooker on high; mix flour with water and add to cooker. Stir until mixture begins to thicken. If you desire a thicker sauce, add more flour-water mixture. Taste and adjust seasonings. Pour sauce over meat and serve.

PORK ADOBO

This is a braised pork dish common in the Philippines. Serve with white rice or more healthful brown rice.

2½ lb. lean pork
salt to taste
¼ cup flour
1 tbs. oil
2-3 cloves garlic, minced
2 medium onions, quartered

2 bay leaves
4 tbs. cider vinegar
1 tbs. soy sauce
¼ cup water
1 tsp. sugar, optional
beaten, fried egg for garnish, optional

Cut fat off pork and cut into 1½-inch cubes. Mix salt and flour together and coat pork cubes. Heat oil in a skillet and fry pork until brown. Add garlic and cook 1 minute. Add onions and bay leaves and cook until onions begin to brown. Transfer ingredients to the slow cooker. Set cooker on low; add remaining ingredients except sugar and egg. Cook for 6 to 8 hours or until pork is tender. Taste and adjust seasonings. Add sugar, if desired. Typically, the garnish is an egg which has been beaten, fried and cut into thin strips.

MARINATED COUNTRY RIBS

Servings: 8

These ribs are precooked with onion and cloves until tender, marinated and then broiled or barbecued.

20-24 country-style spareribs
water to cover meat
1 large whole onion
9 whole cloves
1 tsp. rosemary
1 tsp. thyme
1 tsp. marjoram

1 tsp. oregano
1 cup ketchup
3 tbs. soy sauce
1/3 cup honey
2 cloves garlic, minced
3/4 tsp. ground ginger

Trim excess fat from ribs; place in the slow cooker and cover with water. Stud onion with cloves; add to slow cooker with rosemary, thyme, marjoram and oregano. Set cooker on low and cook 8 to 10 hours or until ribs are tender. Remove ribs; discard liquid and place ribs in a single layer in a shallow pan. Mix together ketchup, soy sauce, honey, garlic and ginger. Spread mixture on both sides of ribs and allow to marinate at room temperature 2 to 3 hours. Leave marinade on ribs and barbecue or broil until browned.

SWEET-AND-SOUR LAMB CHOPS

Servings: 6

An unusual sauce, made with creme de menthe liqueur, is served over broiled or sautéed lamb chops.

2 cups thinly sliced onions
4 tbs. butter
½ cup creme de menthe
½ cup cider or red wine vinegar
2 tbs. sugar
4 tsp. lemon juice
1 cup beef broth
1 tsp. rosemary
6-12 lamb chops, depending on size

Place onions and butter in the slow cooker; set on low and cook for 2 to 3 hours. Add creme de menthe, vinegar, sugar and lemon juice; stir and cook until mixture looks syrupy, about half an hour. Stir in beef broth and rosemary and simmer on low for 45 minutes to 1 hour. Taste and adjust seasoning. Keep sauce warm in slow cooker while broiling or sautéing chops. Pour sauce over lamb chops and serve.

POULTRY ENTRÉES

CRANBERRY CHICKEN

Servings: 4

Cranberries add a slightly tangy flavor to slow-cooked chicken dishes. The berries tend to dissolve so they are not noticeable. With the addition of a little brown sugar the chicken takes on a slightly sweet-and-sour taste. This dish is good served with brown rice.

1 broiler chicken
¾ cup chopped onion
1 cup fresh cranberries
1 tsp. salt
¼ tsp. cinnamon
¼ tsp. ginger

1 tsp. grated orange rind
1 cup orange juice
3 tbs. melted butter
3 tbs. flour
2-3 tbs. brown sugar, optional

Cut chicken into quarters and remove skin. Place in the slow cooker with onion, cranberries, salt, cinnamon, ginger, orange rind and orange juice. Cover and cook on low for 5 to 6 hours. Remove chicken from pot and separate meat from bone; set aside. Mix butter and flour together to form a thick paste. Stir paste into liquid in pot and turn on high to thicken sauce. Add reserved chicken meat and taste. Add brown sugar and any additional seasonings to suit your taste.

CHICKEN CURRY

Ideally, curries should be accompanied with several condiments like chutney, chopped green onions, raisins, chopped nuts, etc. Serve this dish with rice. Coconut milk can be found in large grocery stores, often in the Oriental foods section.

6 whole chicken breasts
water to cover
½ tsp. peppercorns
1 tsp. salt
2 stalks celery, chopped
½ cup butter
1 tbs. oil
2 medium onions, chopped
3 cloves garlic, minced
2 stalks celery, chopped
3 tbs. chopped parsley
1 cucumber, chopped, preferably
  English variety

2 apples, cored, peeled and chopped,
  preferably Golden Delicious
¼ cup flour
1 tsp. nutmeg
1 tsp. dry mustard
3 tbs. curry powder, or to taste
2 cups chicken broth
2 cups cream
1 cup coconut milk
1½ tsp. salt
1 tbs. lemon juice

Split chicken breasts and place in the slow cooker. Add water, peppercorns, salt and celery. Set on low and cook 5 to 6 hours or until chicken is tender. Remove chicken and discard liquid. Debone chicken and cut meat into dice or shred. Set aside. Turn slow cooker on high; heat butter and oil; add onions, garlic, celery, parsley, cucumber and apples. Sauté until tender, stirring frequently. Stir in flour, nutmeg, mustard and curry powder; cook 5 minutes longer. Add chicken broth, cream, coconut milk and salt. Allow mixture to heat up, turn cooker to low and allow sauce to cook for 2 to 3 hours. Press sauce through a sieve. Add lemon juice; taste and adjust seasonings. Transfer chicken to slow cooker and cover with sauce. Heat on low until ready to serve.

CHICKEN EN MOLE

Servings: 8

Mole is a Mexican reddish-brown sauce that has an unusual ingredient, chocolate. The traditional recipe uses finely chopped roasted peanuts, but here it is modernized with peanut butter.

4 cups canned chopped tomatoes
1 large onion, chopped
2 cloves garlic, minced
¾ cup peanut butter
¼ cup tahini, or ground sesame seeds
2 tbs. sugar
1½-2 tbs. chili powder
½ tsp. anise seed
½ tsp. cinnamon
½ tsp. cloves
½ tsp. coriander

½-1 tsp. cumin
2 cups chicken stock
salt and pepper to taste
2 oz. unsweetened chocolate, grated
2 stewing chickens
water to cover
1 tsp. salt
1 tsp. peppercorns
1 tbs. dried onion flakes or ¼ cup
  chopped onion
1 cup chopped celery

Place tomatoes, onion, garlic, peanut butter, tahini, sugar, chili powder, anise, cinnamon, cloves, coriander, cumin, chicken stock, salt and pepper into the slow cooker. Stir; cover; set on low and cook for 6 to 8 hours. Add grated chocolate. Taste and adjust seasonings to your personal preference. You may need to add additional sugar to make mixture slightly sweet.

Cut chicken into pieces and remove skin. Place in a pan and cover with water. Add salt, peppercorns, onion flakes and celery and bring to a boil. Reduce heat; simmer until chicken is tender, 35 to 45 minutes. Remove from heat; separate meat from bone or serve as poached chicken pieces. Cover with mole sauce.

CHUTNEY CHICKEN SALAD

Poaching chicken slowly gives it a succulent quality perfect for salads.

4-5 full chicken breasts
2 bay leaves
1 tsp. salt
$\frac{1}{2}$ tsp. peppercorns
$\frac{1}{2}$ medium onion, coarsely chopped
2 stalks celery, chopped
water to cover
1 cup mayonnaise
$\frac{1}{2}$ cup chopped chutney
1 tsp. curry powder
2 tsp. grated lemon or lime peel
$\frac{1}{4}$ cup lemon or lime juice
$\frac{1}{2}$ tsp. salt
$1\frac{1}{2}$ cups canned pineapple chunks
$\frac{1}{2}$ cup sliced green onions
$1\frac{1}{2}$ cups chopped celery
$\frac{1}{2}$ cup slivered toasted almonds

Cut chicken breasts in half and place in the slow cooker with bay leaves, salt, peppercorns, onion and celery. Cover with water. Set cooker on low and cook for 4 to 6 hours. Take out a chicken piece and cut it in half to make sure chicken is cooked thoroughly. Remove chicken from pot and cool. If you wish, strain vegetables from liquid and save for future use. Dice chicken to make approximately 4 cups chicken meat. Combine mayonnaise, chutney, curry, lemon peel, lemon juice and salt. Toss with chicken; add remaining ingredients except almonds. Chill well. When ready to serve, sprinkle with almonds.

CHICKEN PASTA SALAD

Servings: 6-8

Pasta and succulent poached chicken are very tasty together. This salad stores well and is great for picnics.

3 whole chicken breasts
water to cover
1 stalk celery, chopped
½ large onion, chopped
½ tsp. salt
a few peppercorns
6 oz. dried pasta of choice
½ cup oil
1 tbs. sesame oil

⅓ cup light soy sauce
⅓ cup rice vinegar
3 tbs. sugar
¼ tsp. pepper
½ tsp. ground ginger
¼ cup chopped parsley
⅓ cup sliced green onions
6 cups fresh spinach
¼ cup toasted sesame seeds

Cut chicken breasts in half and place in the slow cooker. Cover with water and add celery, onion, salt and peppercorns. Set on low and cook 5 to 6 hours. When chicken is cooked thoroughly, remove and let cool. Cut into chunks or shred. Cook dried pasta according to package directions until just barely tender (al dente); drain and set aside to cool. In a separate bowl, combine oils, soy sauce, vinegar, sugar, pepper and ginger. Add to chicken and pasta and let marinate for at least 1 hour. Toss in parsley, onions, spinach and sesame seeds. Taste and adjust seasonings and serve.

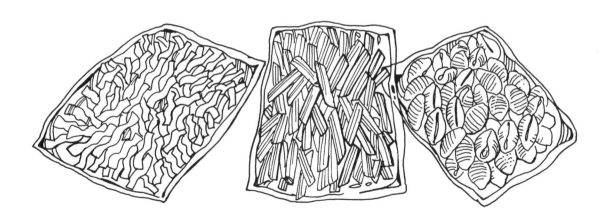

TURKEY LOAF

With the emphasis on low fat meats, ground turkey is a great substitute for ground beef. This recipe uses a unique combination of ingredients for a slightly tangy flavor.

2½ lb. ground turkey
1 medium onion, chopped
2 eggs
⅓ cup milk
2 tbs. prepared horseradish
3 tbs. bottled chili sauce

1 cup bread crumbs
1 tsp. salt
2 cloves garlic, minced
¼ cup minced parsley
sour cream for garnish, optional
capers for garnish, optional

Mix all ingredients except garnishes together. Fry small amount of mixture in a skillet and taste. Adjust seasonings to your personal taste. Place mixture in a pan that fits into the slow cooker (a loaf pan or a 2 lb. coffee can or baking dish if using a round slow cooker). Place a trivet in bottom of cooker and place pan on trivet. Set cooker on low and cook for 7 or 8 hours. Depending on shape of pan, cooking hours may vary. There should be no pink left in meat when it is properly done. Drain off any visible fat. If desired, add a thin layer of sour cream to the top and sprinkle with a few capers.

NECTARINE CHICKEN

I am always looking for new and unique chicken dishes. This dish is incredibly simple to prepare and very low in fat. I like to serve it with brown rice.

$3\frac{1}{2}$ lb. chicken
4-6 nectarines
1 tsp. salt
$\frac{1}{4}$ cup brown sugar
$1\frac{1}{2}$ tsp. ground ginger

$\frac{1}{2}$ tsp. nutmeg
pepper to taste
2 tbs. butter and 2 tbs. flour to thicken, optional

Cut chicken into pieces; remove skin and all visible fat and set aside. Leave peel on nectarines, remove pits and cut into slices. Place chicken in the slow cooker and add remaining ingredients excluding butter and flour. Set on low and cook for 5 to 6 hours. Cooked chicken can be either gently removed and kept on the bone or deboned and returned to pot. Taste and adjust seasonings to your personal preference. The sauce in this recipe is thin. If you prefer thicker sauce, mix butter and flour together to form a paste; stir into hot mixture and allow to thicken gradually. If you left chicken on bone, pour sauce over chicken to serve.

STUFFED CHICKEN ROLLS

Servings: 6

This is a low fat, easy meal that looks and tastes like you spent hours in the kitchen. Serve this with a rice pilaf or simple mashed potatoes.

3 whole chicken breasts
6 thin slices prosciutto or ham
6 thin slices low fat Swiss cheese
flour to coat chicken
½ lb. fresh sliced mushrooms
½ cup chicken stock
½ cup white wine or Marsala wine

¼ tsp. ground rosemary
¼ cup grated Parmesan cheese
2 tsp. cornstarch
1 tbs. water
1 tsp. Kitchen Bouquet
salt and pepper to taste
1 tsp. sugar, optional

Skin and bone chicken breasts and cut in half. Place chicken pieces between 2 pieces of waxed paper and pound until slightly flattened. Place 1 slice of prosciutto and 1 slice of cheese on each breast and roll up. Secure with a toothpick and roll in flour. Put mushrooms in the slow cooker and place chicken rolls on top of mushrooms. In a separate bowl, mix chicken stock, wine and rosemary together and pour over chicken. Sprinkle with Parmesan cheese. Set slow cooker on low and cook for 6 hours. Just before serving, mix cornstarch, water and Kitchen Bouquet together. Remove chicken; add cornstarch mixture and stir until thickened. Add salt, pepper and sugar, if desired. Pour sauce over chicken and serve.

DESSERTS

RASPBERRY BREAD PUDDING

This is a delightful change from the standard bread pudding. Don't limit yourself to raspberries — consider using blackberries, Marion berries, loganberries, etc., for a fruity, warm winter treat.

5 cups toasted bread cubes
2½ cups scalded milk
2 eggs
2 egg yolks
1 cup sugar

1 tsp. almond extract
2 tbs. melted butter
12 oz. fresh or frozen raspberries
whipped cream for garnish

Place toasted bread cubes in the slow cooker. In a separate bowl, mix scalded milk, eggs, egg yolks, sugar, almond extract and melted butter together. Defrost berries; drain off any excess juice and mix berries with bread cubes. Pour milk mixture on top and gently press bread into milk mixture with the back of a spoon. Do not stir mixture. Set slow cooker on low and cook for 4 to 6 hours. Serve warm with a dollop of whipped cream or drizzle with *Raspberry Sauce*, page 107.

RASPBERRY SAUCE

1 pkg. (10 oz.) frozen raspberries
½ cup raspberry jam
few drops lemon juice
sugar, optional
1 tbs. raspberry liqueur, optional

Defrost raspberries. Place raspberries, raspberry jam and lemon juice into a food processor or blender. Puree until smooth; taste and add sugar, if desired. Strain through a sieve to remove seeds. Add raspberry liqueur, if desired. Drizzle sauce over warm *Raspberry Bread Pudding*, page 106.

HOT CHOCOLATE PUDDING

Servings: 8

This is a fudgy, rich chocolate pudding that can be mixed right in the slow cooker. If desired, you can serve with a dollop of whipped cream or a scoop of vanilla ice cream or frozen yogurt.

1½ cups flour
1 cup sugar
3 tbs. unsweetened cocoa powder
1 tbs. baking powder
¾ tsp. salt
¾ cup milk
3 tbs. melted butter
1 tsp. vanilla

¾ cup packed brown sugar
⅓ cup sugar
¼ cup unsweetened cocoa powder
¼ tsp. salt
1½ tsp. vanilla
1½ cups boiling water
¾ cup toasted chopped walnuts,
  optional

Mix flour, sugar, cocoa, baking powder and salt together in the slow cooker. Add milk, butter and vanilla and stir until blended. In a separate bowl, mix sugars, cocoa, salt and vanilla together and sprinkle on top of mixture in slow cooker without stirring. Pour boiling water on top. Do not mix. Set slow cooker on low and cook for 3 hours. If desired, just before serving, add toasted walnuts for texture.

PINEAPPLE BREAD PUDDING

My friend, Joan, brought this recipe to a party and the guests raved, so I adapted the recipe for the slow cooker with a few minor changes. Thanks, Joan!

1 cup softened butter
2 cups sugar
1 tsp. cinnamon
8 eggs
2 cans (13½ oz. each) crushed pineapple
5 cups toasted bread cubes
½ cup chopped toasted pecans
whipped cream for garnish

In a bowl, beat butter, sugar, and cinnamon until well mixed. Add eggs and beat on high until mixture is light and fluffy. Drain pineapple well. Reserve juice for later use. Fold pineapple and bread cubes into creamed mixture. Pour batter into the slow cooker; set cooker on low for 6 to 7 hours. Before serving, sprinkle pecans on top of pudding and serve warm with a dollop of whipped cream. Serve warm.

BREAD PUDDING

This easy-to-make bread pudding reminds me of the kind of homey food my grandmother used to make on cold, wintry days.

4 cups toasted bread cubes
2½ cups scalded milk
2 eggs
¾ cup sugar
¼ tsp. cinnamon
pinch nutmeg

pinch salt
1 tsp. vanilla
2 tbs. melted butter
½ cup raisins, optional
whipped cream for garnish

Put bread cubes in the slow cooker. In a separate container, mix scalded milk, eggs, sugar, cinnamon, nutmeg, salt, vanilla and melted butter. Pour mixture over bread cubes and add raisins, if desired. With the back of a spoon, gently press all bread cubes into milk mixture to make sure liquid is absorbed. Avoid stirring mixture so bread does not disintegrate. Set cooker on low and cook for 5 to 6 hours. Serve warm with a dollop of whipped cream, if desired.

APPLE BREAD PUDDING

Apples give bread pudding a delightful moistness and delicious flavor. I toast the bread before cooking to give it a nutty flavor. Serve with whipped cream, ice cream, frozen yogurt or other favorite topping.

8-9 pieces white or egg bread
4 tbs. butter
3 apples, preferably Golden Delicious
2 tbs. lemon juice
1 tbs. grated lemon rind
$\frac{1}{2}$-1 cup brown sugar

1 tsp. cinnamon
$\frac{1}{4}$ tsp. nutmeg
1 cup apple juice
$\frac{1}{2}$ cup golden raisins
$\frac{1}{2}$ cup toasted walnuts, optional

Spread bread with butter and toast both sides under a broiler. Cut bread into chunks. Place all ingredients in the slow cooker except walnuts. The amount of sugar should be determined by tartness of apples. Set slow cooker on low and allow to cook for 5 to 6 hours. If possible, gently stir halfway through cooking process. If desired, stir in toasted walnuts just before serving.

CHOCOLATE WALNUT BROWNIES

Servings: 12

When you don't have access to an oven, you can bake with your slow cooker. These are great, moist brownies that are not extremely sweet.

½ cup butter
1 cup sugar
4 eggs
1 tsp. vanilla
1 can (16 oz.) chocolate syrup
1 cup flour
½ tsp. baking powder
1 cup chopped walnuts
2 cups water

Cream butter and sugar together. Add eggs, vanilla, chocolate syrup, flour and baking powder; beat well. Stir in walnuts. Use a coffee tin for a standard round cooker, or a loaf pan for a rectangular-shaped cooker. Grease baking pan well and pour in chocolate mixture. Set a trivet in the bottom of the slow cooker; place baking pan on top of trivet and cover pan with several layers of paper towel. Pour water into cooker. Set slow cooker on high and cook for approximately 3 to 4 hours.

Depending on depth of pan used for baking and type of cooker, time may vary, so check every 15 minutes after 3-hour period for doneness. When cool, cut brownies into long slices; frost. If desired, sprinkle with additional walnuts.

CHOCOLATE FROSTING

1 cup powdered sugar
1/4 cup butter
1/3 cup milk
1/2 cup chocolate chips

Heat powdered sugar, butter and milk in a saucepan and stir until sugar is dissolved. Remove from heat; stir in chocolate chips and beat until smooth. Spread on cooled brownies.

APPLE INDIAN PUDDING

Servings: 8

Indian pudding is an old-fashioned cornmeal pudding that is strongly flavored with molasses. Apples add texture and moistness and give this dessert real substance. This is a great finale to a traditional meat and potatoes meal.

2 cups milk
1/3 cup cornmeal
2 cups sliced apples, preferably Golden
  Delicious
3/4 cup molasses
1/4 cup melted butter
1 tsp. salt

1 tsp. ginger
1/2 tsp. cinnamon
3 tbs. sugar
1 beaten egg
1/2 cup light or dark raisins
whipped cream for garnish

Bring milk to a boil in a saucepan and add cornmeal. Place mixture in the slow cooker and add remaining ingredients. Amount of sugar varies depending on the type of apples used. Set slow cooker on low and cook for 4 to 5 hours. Allow pudding to cool to room temperature before serving as it will thicken as it cools. Since pudding is a dark brown color, I would suggest serving it with a dollop of whipped cream, ice cream or frozen yogurt.

CRANBERRY PUDDING

*This is similar to steamed plum pudding, but more colorful and fresher tasting. If you freeze fresh cranberries when they are plentiful, you can have this dessert year-round. Top with **Butter Sauce**, page 121, or **Hard Sauce**, page 117.*

2 cups fresh or defrosted frozen cranberries
1½ cups flour
½ cup molasses, preferably light
½ cup boiling water
2 tsp. baking soda
¼ tsp. salt
1 tsp. grated orange rind

Coarsely chop cranberries and mix with flour (this helps prevent the berries from sinking to the bottom of the pudding during steaming). Mix molasses, water, soda, salt and orange rind together; stir into cranberries.

Grease a pudding mold or large coffee tin, pour in pudding mixture, cover with waxed paper and tie tightly with a string. Place in the slow cooker and pour water in to fill halfway up mold. Set cooker on high and cook for 5 to 6 hours. Check doneness by inserting knife in center. It should come out clean. Serve warm or at room temperature.

HOLIDAY PLUM PUDDING

This is a traditional English plum pudding which is dark with spices and rich with fruits. If candied citron is not a favorite ingredient, try substituting candied cherries or even chopped maraschino cherries. For a delightful alternative, consider flavoring the hard sauce with different liqueurs.

granulated sugar for dusting
8 oz. pitted dates
8 oz. dried figs
8 oz. dried apricots
8 oz. walnuts
15 oz. raisins
4 oz. chopped candied citron, or
  candied cherries
1 cup sifted flour

1 tbs. pumpkin pie spice
1 tsp. salt
4 eggs
1 cup packed brown sugar
$\frac{1}{2}$ lb. ground suet
$2\frac{1}{2}$ cups soft white bread crumbs
$\frac{1}{2}$ cup brandy
$\frac{1}{2}$ cup corn syrup

Butter a 10-cup mold or large coffee tin and dust with granulated sugar, tapping out any excess. Chop dates, figs, apricots and walnuts into small pieces and combine with raisins and candied citron in a large bowl. Mix flour, pumpkin pie spice and salt together and set aside. With an electric mixer, beat eggs and brown sugar together at high speed for 3 minutes until fluffy. Lower speed and mix in suet, bread crumbs, brandy and corn syrup. Stir in flour mixture until well blended. Pour mixture over fruit and nut mixture; stir until well blended. Spoon into prepared mold, cover with foil and fasten with string. Place mold in the slow cooker and fill cooker with water to halfway up mold. Set cooker on high and cook 6 to 7 hours. Test for doneness by inserting a skewer in center of pudding. It should come out clean. Cool pudding in mold for 30 minutes before removing. Serve warm or at room temperature with sauce.

TRADITIONAL HARD SAUCE

½ cup butter
2 cups powdered sugar
¼ tsp. salt
2 tbs. brandy, rum or whiskey, or more to taste

With an electric beater or food processor, beat butter until smooth. Sift powdered sugar and add to butter, beating well. Add salt and chosen liquor. Add additional liquor, if desired. Chill until ready to use, but bring to room temperature before serving.

FRUITED HARD SAUCE

This makes a delightful alternative to hard sauce over a holiday pudding.

⅔ cups butter
2¼ cups powdered sugar
½ cup cream
1⅓ cup crushed berries, chopped maraschino cherries or mashed bananas
1 tbs. berry-flavored liqueur, amaretto or banana liqueur, optional

With an electric mixer or food processor, beat butter until smooth. Sift powdered sugar and add to butter, beating well. Beat in cream and add crushed fruit, beating well. If desired, beat in a liqueur that complements fruit used. Chill.

SPICY HARD SAUCE

This can be used instead of a traditional hard sauce over a holiday pudding.

$\frac{1}{2}$ cup butter
2 cups powdered sugar
$\frac{1}{4}$ tsp. salt
1 tsp. cinnamon
$\frac{1}{2}$ tsp. cloves
pinch nutmeg
$\frac{1}{2}$ cup cream
1-2 tbs. liquor or liqueur of choice

With an electric mixer or food processor, beat butter until soft. Sift powdered sugar and add to butter, beating well. Add remaining ingredients, beating well. Chill.

SIMPLE FUDGE SAUCE

Makes: 1 quart

*This easy fudge sauce can be used as a dessert fondue for dipping bananas, angel food cake, pound cake, etc. It also can be used as a delicious sauce over ice cream or cake. For a special treat, use this sauce as a base for **Chocolate Almond Truffles**, page 124.*

12 oz. semi-sweet chocolate chips
¼ cup butter
2 cans (14 oz. each) sweetened condensed milk
⅓ cup liqueur — amaretto, orange-flavored, Frangelico, coffee or mint, optional

Place chocolate chips, butter and condensed milk in the slow cooker. Turn cooker on low and cook for 1 to 2 hours; stir occasionally until chocolate melts . Stir in liqueur, if desired. Serve directly from slow cooker or serve warm over desserts. Store covered in the refrigerator for up to 2 weeks.

BUTTER SAUCE

*This is delicious over **Cranberry Pudding**, page 115.*

1 cup sugar
½ cup butter
½ cup cream
1 tsp. vanilla or grated orange peel

In a heavy-bottomed saucepan or double boiler, slowly heat sugar, butter and cream until sugar is dissolved. Using an electric mixer, whip at high speed until thickened. Stir in vanilla or grated orange peel.

FILLED PEARS IN WINE

This is a popular, light dessert made even more special with a delicious filling.

6 firm Danjou or Bosc pears
2 cups dry red wine
1 cup sugar
1 tsp. grated lemon rind
1½ tsp. cornstarch
1 tbs. water

½ cup chopped almonds
1 tbs. sugar
½ cup crushed macaroons, vanilla
  wafers or toasted ladyfingers
whipped cream for garnish

Peel pears, cut a thin slice from the bottoms so they stand up by themselves and place them in the slow cooker. Mix together wine, sugar and lemon rind and pour over pears. Set slow cooker on low and cook for 4 to 6 hours. To test for doneness, pears should be easy to pierce with a sharp knife but not mushy. Remove pears and allow to cool. Turn cooker on high. Mix cornstarch with water. When wine mixture begins to bubble, add cornstarch mixture and stir until thickened. Mix almonds, sugar and crushed macaroons together. When pears are cool enough to handle, core pears with an apple corer, leaving pears whole. Drizzle with glaze. You may have to glaze several times to achieve a thick coating on pears. Carefully fill pears with almond-macaroon mixture. Serve with a dollop of whipped cream.

ORANGE FONDUE

Don't be limited in thinking dessert fondues can only be chocolate. This is a creamy, simple dessert that can be served with fresh fruit, canned fruit or cake.

$\frac{1}{4}$ cup butter
$\frac{1}{4}$ cup flour
$1\frac{1}{2}$ cups half-and-half
$\frac{1}{4}$ cup sugar
1 tbs. grated orange peel
8 oz. cream cheese
$\frac{1}{2}$ cup orange-flavored liqueur, optional

In the slow cooker on high, melt butter and whisk in flour to form a paste. Slowly stir in half-and-half until smooth. Add sugar and orange peel and stir. Turn slow cooker on low. Cube cream cheese and stir into cream mixture. Cook on low, stirring occasionally, until cream cheese melts, about 1 hour. Stir in liqueur, if desired.

CHOCOLATE ALMOND TRUFFLES

Servings: 6

When I allowed the fudge sauce recipe to cool to room temperature, it solidified into the consistency of a truffle. Consider using mint, Frangelico or orange liqueurs for flavorings.

1 recipe *Simple Fudge Sauce*, page 119
amaretto liqueur or almond flavoring, to taste
1 cup finely chopped toasted almonds

Allow fudge sauce to come to room temperature and solidify. Add amaretto and stir. Using a small ice cream scoop or melon baller, scoop out chocolate into balls about walnut size. Drop onto a plate with finely chopped toasted almonds and roll, coating each ball thoroughly. Refrigerate until ready to serve.

APPLE DATE PUDDING

This delicious, easy-to-fix, warm dessert can be topped with whipped cream or ice cream.

4-5 apples, peeled, cored and diced
3/4 cup sugar, or less, to taste
1/2 cup chopped dates
1/2 cup toasted, chopped pecans
2 tbs. flour

1 tsp. baking powder
1/8 tsp. salt
1/4 tsp. nutmeg
2 tbs. melted butter
1 egg, beaten

In the slow cooker, place apples, sugar, dates and pecans; stir. In a separate bowl, mix together flour, baking powder, salt and nutmeg and stir into apple mixture. Drizzle melted butter over batter and stir. Stir in egg. Set cooker on low and cook for 3 to 4 hours. Serve warm.

NOTE: If crispier nuts are desired, add toasted pecans at the end of cooking period.

APRICOTS IN ALMOND LIQUEUR

Servings: 6

This is a quick and simple dessert that is delightful after a heavy meal.

1 can (19 oz.) whole apricots
1 tbs. cornstarch
½ cup amaretto liqueur
whipped cream for garnish
toasted slivered almonds for garnish

Drain apricots and place juice in the slow cooker with cornstarch. Stir to dissolve. Turn cooker on low and allow mixture to thicken, half an hour to 1 hour. Add amaretto and cook half an hour longer. Pour sauce over apricots; cover and refrigerate for several hours. Garnish with whipped cream and a sprinkling of toasted almonds.

THIS AND THAT:

CEREALS AND GRAINS; RELISHES AND SAUCES; POTPOURRI

OAT GROATS

This is a favorite hot breakfast cereal my mother used to serve. It is the whole oat kernel which contains all the natural fiber and nutrition. Put this cereal in the slow cooker just before going to bed and awaken to a delicious, chewy cereal.

1 cup oat groats
1 tsp. salt
4 cups water
pinch cinnamon or nutmeg, raisins, chopped dates, and/or chopped toasted
  nuts, optional

Place oat groats, salt, water, and any of the optional ingredients in the slow cooker and stir. Set on low and allow it to cook for 8 to 10 hours.

NOTE: There may be a skin on top of the cereal; if so, simply remove it with a spoon. Do not stir it into the cereal.

KAMUT CEREAL

Kamut (say KAH-MOOT) is a highly nutritious wheat that contains a unique type of gluten easier for the body to utilize. Its grains are up to three times larger than wheat. It has more protein and potassium than wheat and it has a nutty, buttery flavor.

3 cups water
½ tsp. salt
1 cup whole grain kamut
pinch cinnamon or nutmeg, raisins or chopped dates, grated orange rind, optional
chopped toasted nuts, optional

Place water, salt and kamut in the slow cooker and add any optional ingredients as desired. If you add nuts, do so after cooking so they won't become soggy. Set cooker on low and cook for 8 to 9 hours.

PARMESAN POLENTA

Servings: 6-8

Polenta is a delicious alternative to potatoes or rice. It is simple to fix and can be chilled in loaf form to serve sliced with a tomato sauce.

2 cups polenta
6 cups boiling water
1 tsp. salt, or to taste
¼ cup butter
1 cup grated Parmesan cheese, preferably Asiago

Place polenta in the slow cooker; pour boiling water on top and stir. Add remaining ingredients and stir. Set cooker on low and cook for 1 to 2 hours, stirring occasionally until mixture thickens and is smooth and soft.

If you wish to serve polenta with a sauce, butter a loaf pan; pour in hot polenta and refrigerate until firm. Cut solid polenta into slices, place on a platter, heat in the oven until warm and top with *Basil Tomato Sauce*, page 131.

BASIL TOMATO SAUCE

Makes: 3 cups

This is a fast simple sauce, made special with the addition of fresh basil.

¼ cup olive oil
3 cloves garlic, minced
2¼ cups canned plum tomatoes
salt and pepper to taste
15 fresh basil leaves, or 2 tsp. dried basil

Heat oil in a saucepan and gently fry garlic on medium until just golden but not brown. Chop tomatoes into small pieces, add to saucepan and cook on low, uncovered, until oil floats free on top. Add salt, pepper and basil. If using fresh basil, take sauce off heat and stir in chopped fresh basil leaves. Taste and adjust seasonings.

JALAPEÑO GRITS

Grits can be quite plain, but with the addition of jalapeño cheese you get spectacular results. Use this as a starch in place of potatoes, rice or pasta — but be aware that this dish is very rich.

4 cups boiling water
1 cup dried corn grits
dash of salt
½ cup butter
1 tube (8 oz.) jalapeño cheese
2 beaten eggs
1½ tsp. seasoning salt

In the slow cooker, pour boiling water over corn grits and stir until smooth. Turn cooker on low and allow grits to sit in cooker for 5 to 10 minutes before adding remaining ingredients. Stir until butter melts. Cook for 3 to 4 hours. Taste and adjust seasoning.

APPLE CRANBERRY RELISH

Makes: 12 cups

Here in the Pacific Northwest where apples grow in abundance, we add apples to recipes for sweetness and sometimes tartness. This recipe can be varied by adding spices like cinnamon, cloves, allspice and/or nutmeg to give it more of a chutney flavor.

8 cups apples, peeled and sliced
12 oz. fresh cranberries
1 cup boiling water
2 cups sugar
1/4 cup cornstarch

Place apples, cranberries, boiling water and 1 cup sugar in the slow cooker, set on low and cook for 4 to 6 hours. Mix remaining 1 cup sugar and cornstarch together and stir into cranberry mixture. Cook until sugar is dissolved and juice is clear. Cool and refrigerate until ready to serve.

CRANBERRY CHUTNEY

Makes: 8 cups

Slow cookers are great for highly spiced fruit dishes like compotes and chutneys. Cranberry chutneys are best served with poultry and pork entrées and, of course, curry dishes.

4 cups fresh cranberries
1 cup water
½ cup golden raisins
½ cup dark raisins
2 cups sugar
1 tsp. ginger
1 tsp. cinnamon
½ tsp. allspice
pinch cloves
½ tsp. salt
1 can (20 oz.) crushed pineapple, drained

Place all ingredients in the slow cooker and stir. Set cooker on low and cook for 4 to 6 hours. Taste and adjust seasonings.

NECTARINE CHUTNEY

Makes: 2 quarts

A fruit chutney like this goes well with Indian curries, as well as meat and fowl dishes. It can also be added to other sauces to bring out an unusual spiciness.

2½ lb. nectarines, peeled, pitted and sliced
1½ cups brown sugar
1 cup cider vinegar
¼ cup diced preserved ginger
1 tbs. salt, or to taste
¼ cup chopped onion
1 tsp. dry mustard
¼ tsp. cinnamon
⅛ tsp. cloves
½ cup slivered almonds, toasted

Place nectarines in the slow cooker with brown sugar, vinegar, ginger, salt, onion, mustard, cinnamon and cloves. Stir mixture well, set cooker on low and cook for 3 to 4 hours or until thick. Taste and adjust seasoning. Let chutney cool. Add almonds and refrigerate until ready to use. If desired, place mixture in a sterilized jar and process to heat seal.

PEACH PINEAPPLE CHUTNEY

Makes: 10 cups

Chutney is certainly becoming more popular, especially with increased interest in Indian cooking. This chutney goes well with wild game, lamb, curries, turkey, chicken, pork or even ham.

5 cups peeled fruits — peaches,
  pineapple and apples
1 lemon, thinly sliced and seeded
2 cloves garlic, chopped
2¼ cups brown sugar

¾ cup crystallized ginger, chopped
2 tsp. salt
½ tsp. cayenne, or more to taste
2 cups cider vinegar
1 cup raisins, mixed dark and light

Mix any proportion of fruits and chop coarsely. Cut lemon slices into quarters and add to the slow cooker with fruits. Add remaining ingredients; set cooker on low and cook for 4 to 6 hours. Stir occasionally to prevent scorching. After cooling, keep refrigerated until ready to use. If you choose to can, process for 5 minutes in a water bath after ladling into sterile jars.

NOTE: Ginger already adds heat to your recipe so be careful with the amount of cayenne.

HEALTHY APPLE BUTTER

Makes: 4 cups

For health-minded people, this recipe is sugarless, salt-free and fat-free. What more could you ask for?

8 lb. apples, peeled, cored and diced
1½ cups apple juice
2 tsp. cinnamon
1 tsp. nutmeg, or more to taste

Place apples in a blender or food processor with apple juice and blend until smooth. Transfer to the slow cooker, set on low and cook for 6 to 7 hours. Stir occasionally. Let mixture cool; reblend and stir in spices. If desired, add more spices to taste. Store in the refrigerator after cooling to room temperature.

PEAR HONEY

Makes: 1½-2 quarts

Pear honey is a spread something like apple butter that can be used on toast, crumpets, muffins, etc.

15 pears, peeled and cored
3 whole oranges
3 tbs. lemon juice
1 can (20 oz.) crushed pineapple
3-4 cups sugar, or more to taste

Use pears that are not overly ripe. Cut pears into chunks. Slice oranges, with peel left on, and remove seeds. In a food processor or blender, puree both fruits. Place all ingredients in the slow cooker and cook for 4 to 6 hours or until thick. Taste and add more sugar, if desired. Amount of sugar may vary considerably depending on ripeness of pears. Store in the refrigerator.

PEANUT SAUCE (SATÉ SAUCE)

(Say SAH-TAY.) This sauce is popular to serve with Thai marinated chicken or beef skewers. It's also good over lightly sautéed chicken and fresh spinach.

¼ cup oil
2 cloves garlic, minced
1 medium onion, chopped
½ tsp. chili powder
3 lime leaves
½ tsp. curry powder
1 tbs. chopped lemon grass
1 cup coconut milk
½ cup milk

¼ tsp. cinnamon
3 bay leaves
2 tsp. tamarind paste or 1 tbs. lemon juice
2 tbs. fish sauce
3 tbs. dark brown sugar
3 tbs. lemon juice
1 cup chunky peanut butter

Turn the slow cooker on high. Heat oil and add garlic, onion, chili powder, lime leaves, curry powder and lemon grass. Cook until onion is tender. Turn cooker on low and stir in remaining ingredients. Cook on low for 2 to 3 hours or until thick.

NOTE: Fish sauce is available in Asian markets.

SPICED APPLESAUCE

Makes: 6 cups

Applesauce is becoming more popular as a substitute for high sugar sauces and syrups. A favorite alternative is to use applesauce on pancakes in the place of syrup. You can play with the spices for more variety.

12 apples, peeled, cored and sliced
½ cup sugar, or more to taste
2 tbs. lemon juice
1 tsp. grated lemon rind
1 stick (4-6 inch) cinnamon*
½ tsp. nutmeg
¼ tsp. allspice
pinch cloves

Place all ingredients in the slow cooker and set on low. Cook for approximately 4 to 6 hours or until apples are tender. The time will vary depending on the type of apples used. Remove cinnamon stick. Taste and adjust seasonings. Serve warm or cold.

* I generally like to use a cinnamon stick because it doesn't darken the sauce as much, but you can substitute ½ tsp. cinnamon, or more, if you wish.

SWEET-AND-SOUR APRICOT SAUCE

Makes: 2 quarts

This sauce is excellent for poultry, pork and lamb dishes or as an accompaniment to Chinese dishes. When apricots are plentiful, make a large batch and process for future use.

6 cups pitted, chopped apricots
1 cup light raisins
2 cups brown sugar
1 tsp. cinnamon
1/2 tsp. cloves
1/2 tsp. allspice

2 tsp. salt
1/4-1/2 tsp. cayenne, optional
2 large onions, chopped
4 cloves garlic, minced
24 oz. Japanese preserved ginger
1 1/2 cups cider vinegar

Place apricots, raisins, brown sugar, cinnamon, cloves, allspice, salt and cayenne, if desired in the slow cooker and set on low. In a food processor or blender, puree onions, garlic, ginger and vinegar until smooth. Add onion mixture to slow cooker and stir. Cook for 3 to 4 hours, stirring occasionally, until mixture is thick like ketchup. Taste and adjust seasonings. Store in the refrigerator until ready to use or process in sterilized jars to heat seal.

RHUBARB STRAWBERRY SAUCE

Makes: 2 cups

This sauce can be served over ice cream, crepes or chocolate desserts.

8 oz. rhubarb
water to cover
8 oz. strawberries
$\frac{1}{2}$ cup sugar, or to taste
2 tbs. lemon juice
1 tsp. grated lemon peel

Slice rhubarb and place in the slow cooker with enough water to cover. Set cooker on low and cook for 1 hour or until rhubarb is tender. Strain liquid from rhubarb and puree cooked rhubarb until smooth. Add strawberries, sugar, lemon juice and peel. Puree until well mixed and smooth. Taste and adjust sweetness or tartness to personal preference.

CHILI SAUCE

This is a quick easy sauce that can be served over kebabs, fish dishes, pasta, potatoes, or even as garnish to soups and stews.

1/2 cup olive oil
6 large onions, chopped
12 cloves garlic
3/4 cup chopped red chili peppers
1 1/2 cups ketchup
salt to taste, optional

In a skillet, heat oil and sauté onions until soft. Mince garlic; seed and chop peppers and add both to onion mixture. Transfer to a food processor or blender and puree with ketchup. Place all ingredients in the slow cooker and cook on low for 45 minutes to 1 hour. Taste and adjust seasonings.

PRUNE SAUCE

Makes: 1 quart

For a delightful change, try this unique sauce on roast pork or poultry dishes.

14 oz. pitted prunes
¼ cup lemon juice
2 tbs. grated lemon peel
18 whole cloves
¼ tsp. cinnamon
¼ tsp. allspice
1 tsp. nutmeg
2 cups water, approximately
1 cup sugar
1 cup vinegar, preferably balsamic

Place prunes, lemon juice, lemon peel, cloves, cinnamon, allspice and nutmeg in the slow cooker and add enough water to just cover. Cook on low for 45 minutes to 1 hour, until prunes are soft. When liquid has been reduced to about half the original amount, remove cloves and puree mixture in a food processor or blender. Return to slow cooker; add sugar and vinegar and cook on low until sugar dissolves and mixture is smooth. Taste and adjust seasoning.

CHOCOLATE ESPRESSO SAUCE

This is a rich, not overly sweet sauce which is great for dipping cakes or fruit or as a topping for ice cream. My favorite use is to make ice cream mud pies with mocha-flavored ice cream.

12 oz. unsweetened chocolate, finely chopped
2⅔ cups hot espresso coffee
3 cups sugar
½ cup amaretto liqueur
½ cup butter

Put chocolate in the slow cooker. Mix espresso coffee and sugar together, pour over chocolate and stir. Turn slow cooker on low and cook until chocolate is melted and smooth, stirring occasionally, about 45 minutes to 1 hour. Add amaretto and butter; stir until smooth and glossy. Serve over ice cream or keep warm and use as a dessert fondue. This sauce can also be allowed to cool and used with ice cream pie or frozen desserts.

HOT CRANBERRY SAUCE

Instead of opening a can and serving a cold cranberry sauce to accompany poultry or pork dishes, you may consider a hot sauce that can be spiked with a little wine or liquor.

2 cups fresh cranberries
3½ cups cranberry juice cocktail
3 tbs. cornstarch
½ cup packed brown sugar
¼ cup lemon juice
½ cup fruity red wine, whiskey or bourbon, optional

Place cranberries and half of cranberry juice cocktail in the slow cooker on high. Cook until berries begin to burst, 1 to 2 hours. Dissolve cornstarch in remaining cranberry juice cocktail. Add dissolved cornstarch, brown sugar and lemon juice to mixture in cooker and turn to low. Cook until mixture begins to thicken. Turn cooker off. Add wine. Taste and adjust seasonings. Serve warm.

FRUIT COMPOTE

Makes: 7 cups

Use this wonderful compote to serve with meat, game, poultry and even fish.

1 cup dried prunes
water to cover
1 cup canned peaches, drained
1 cup canned pears, drained
1 cup canned apricots, drained
3 cups applesauce
2 tbs. lemon juice
1 tbs. grated lemon peel
2 tsp. cinnamon
1 tsp. ginger
1 tsp. nutmeg

Place dried prunes in the slow cooker with water and set cooker on high. Cook for 1 hour or until prunes are soft. Drain off water and add remaining ingredients. Set cooker on low and cook for 2 to 3 hours. Taste and adjust seasonings.

SPICY POTPOURRI

Makes: 2½ quarts

This is not to eat, but to fill your house full of a spicy aroma of cloves, cinnamon and nutmeg — ideal for the holidays.

8 cups dried rose petals
2 cups dried lavender flowers
2 tsp. anise seed
2 tbs. whole cloves
2 tbs. nutmeg
2 tbs. coarsely crushed cinnamon stick

2 tbs. crushed fixative, preferably
  benzoin*
10 drops jasmine oil
10 drops rose geranium oil
10 drops patchouli oil
10 drops rosemary oil

Mix all ingredients together well and place in a dark container or preferably store in glass in a dark cupboard. Allow to season for 1 month before using.

Fill the slow cooker half full of water. Toss in 1 or 2 cups of seasoned potpourri. Heat on low and leave lid off cooker. The aroma will fill your house and help create a holiday memory.

*The flower oils used are essential volatile oils that can be obtained from craft stores, health food stores, etc. Fixatives are used to maintain the fragrance of the ingredients. They absorb the oils and retard evaporation. Fixatives like benzoin or tonka bean are available at craft stores or floral shops.

LAVENDER POTPOURRI

Makes: 2¼ lb.

This potpourri is delicate and reminiscent of "the olden days." Besides using it in the slow cooker as a room freshener, this mix can be used to fill sachets.

1 lb. dried lavender flowers
2 oz. dried sweet woodruff
1½ oz. dried thyme
1½ oz. dried moss, any fragrant variety
8 oz. slivered orange peel
½ cup crushed benzoin fixative *
2 oz. dried violet flowers
1 tbs. whole cloves
1 tbs. anise seed

Mix all ingredients together well. Place in a dark container or preferably store in glass in a dark place. Allow to season for 1 month.

Fill the slow cooker half full of water and toss in 1 to 2 cups of potpourri mix. Heat on low without the lid, allowing the house to fill with this delightful aroma.

* Floral fixatives (like benzoin) can be found at craft or floral stores.

INDEX

SERVE CREATIVE, EASY, NUTRITIOUS MEALS WITH nitty gritty® COOKBOOKS

Edible Pockets for Every Meal
Cooking With Chile Peppers
Oven and Rotisserie Roasting
Risottos, Paellas and Other Rice
  Specialties
Entrées From Your Bread Machine
Muffins, Nut Breads and More
Healthy Snacks for Kids
100 Dynamite Desserts
Recipes for Yogurt Cheese
Sautés
Cooking in Porcelain
Appetizers
Casseroles
The Best Bagels are made at home*
  (*perfect for your bread machine)
The Toaster Oven Cookbook
Skewer Cooking on the Grill
Creative Mexican Cooking
Extra-Special Crockery Pot Recipes
Slow Cooking
Cooking in Clay
Marinades
Deep Fried Indulgences

Cooking with Parchment Paper
The Garlic Cookbook
From Your Ice Cream Maker
Cappuccino/Espresso: The Book of
  Beverages
The Best Pizza is made at home*
  (*perfect for your bread machine)
The Well Dressed Potato
Convection Oven Cookery
The Steamer Cookbook
The Pasta Machine Cookbook
The Versatile Rice Cooker
The Dehydrator Cookbook
The Bread Machine Cookbook
The Bread Machine Cookbook II
The Bread Machine Cookbook III
The Bread Machine Cookbook IV:
  Whole Grains and Natural Sugars
The Bread Machine Cookbook V:
  Favorite Recipes from 100 Kitchens
The Bread Machine Cookbook VI:
  *Hand-Shaped Breads from the
  Dough Cycle*

Worldwide Sourdoughs From Your
  Bread Machine
Recipes for the Pressure Cooker
The New Blender Book
The Sandwich Maker Cookbook
Waffles
Indoor Grilling
The Coffee Book
The Juicer Books I and II
Bread Baking (traditional)
No Salt, No Sugar, No Fat Cookbook
Cooking for 1 or 2
Quick and Easy Pasta Recipes
The 9x13 Pan Cookbook
Recipes for the Loaf Pan
Low Fat American Favorites
Now That's Italian!
Healthy Cooking on the Run
The Wok
Favorite Seafood Recipes
New International Fondue Cookbook
Favorite Cookie Recipes
Flatbreads From Around the World

For a free catalog, write or call:
Bristol Publishing Enterprises, Inc.
P.O. Box 1737, San Leandro, CA 94577
(800) 346-4889; in California, (510) 895-4461